Historic Landscapes
Summit County, Colorado
Ghost Towns and Townsites

Volume 3

Conger's Camp, Dyersville, and More

By
Bill Fountain
Sandra Mather, PhD

Copyright © 2024 Summit Historical Society

All Rights Reserved. No portion of this book may be reproduced in any form or by any electronic or mechanical means, including information storage and retrieval systems, without permission from the publisher, except by a reviewer who may quote brief passages in review.

Published in the United States of American by Summit Historical Society Press,
103 Labonte Street, P.O. Box 143, Dillon, Colorado 80435

www.summithistorical.org

Historic Landscapes, Summit County, Colorado,
Ghost Towns and Townsites,
Volume 3: Conger's Camp, Dyersville, and More

Authors: Bill Fountain and Sandra F. Mather, PhD
Editors: Bill Fountain and Sandra F. Mather, PhD

1st edition: May 15, 2024

ISBN: 978-1-943829-58-3
Library of Congress Control Number 2024915728
Summit Historical Society Press is an imprint of Rhyolite Press LLC,
P.O. Box 60144, Colorado Springs, CO 80960.

This book is sponsored by Tom and Ginger.

Cover Photos:
Top: Remains of Dyersville, 1961

Bottom trio L to R:
Remains of Hotel in Quandary City, 1953
El Dorado Mill, Monte Cristo Gulch, 1890s
Remains of Columbine Shaft, Warrior's Mark Mine, 1971

Book Design & Layout: Marla Morelos

Dedication

For many years, a group of people working individually and collaboratively has investigated, documented, and interpreted the historic landscapes of Breckenridge and Summit County— collecting photographs, documents, and artifacts for the benefit of future generations; writing books, monographs, and newspaper articles; leading field experiences; presenting special programs; and sharing their expertise willingly whenever asked.

Larry Crispell, Mary Ellen Gilliland, Leigh Girvin, Rick Hague, Kris Ann Knish, Maureen Nicholls, Larissa O'Neil, Bob Schoppe, Rich Skovlin, Robin Theobald, Eric Twitty, Wendy Wolfe—to you we dedicate this series of books and say thank you and Mahalo.

TABLE OF CONTENTS

Acknowledgements 6

Prologue 7

Chapter 1 9
Bloomfield

Chapter 2 13
Silver Lake

Chapter 3 45
Quandary City

Chapter 4 63
Conger's Camp/Argentine

Chapter 5 81
Warrenville

Chapter 6 85
Dyersville

Bibliography 156

Index 158

About the Authors 160

Acknowledgements

As with any publication, certain individuals, governmental agencies, and other entities provided vital assistance, support, and encouragement. Our thanks go to Maureen Nicholls, Robin Theobald, Ed and Nancy (deceased) Bathke, Rich Skovlin, Rick Hague, Larissa O'Neil, Kris Ann Knish, Robert Phillippi, Ben Brewer, Greg Thompson, the Breckenridge History Archives, the Summit Historical Society, History Colorado, Mansfield Library at the University of Montana in Missoula, Summit County Clerk and Recorder's Office, and the Bureau of Land Management in Lakewood, Colorado.

Much of the research comes from the Colorado Historic Newspaper Collection website (www.coloradohistoricnewspapers.org). The *Summit County Journal*, the *Breckenridge Bulletin*, and the *Summit County Journal and Breckenridge Bulletin* (The two merged for almost five years beginning in October, 1909.) are available online from 1892 until early 1923.

A special thanks goes to Jerry Eggleston and Richard Frajola for allowing us to use postcards and postmarked envelopes from their collection.

We extend heartfelt gratitude to Eric Twitty, owner of Mountain States Historical, for granting us special permission to quote and use maps from his Colorado Cultural Resource Survey. His research and writing truly enhanced the quality of our manuscript.

The aerial photographs at the end of the chapters came from Google Earth.

A very special thank you to Mike Shipley, CEO of Key Media, who offered the services of his company in laying out not only this book but all seven in this series. Mike owns the Country Boy Mine in French Gulch near Breckenridge, which draws tourists and residents alike to experience an authentic late 1800s mine. Mike also supported the publication of the book, *Country Boy Mine, Breckenridge, Colorado, 1881 – 1994,* by Fountain and Mather.

Also, many thanks to Marla Morelos, Head of Graphic Design for Key Media, for preparing the layout. She has become a treasured colleague.

Prologue

Why *Historic Landscapes, Summit County, Colorado*? Bill Fountain explains: My idea of writing a book about the historic towns of Summit County found from Hoosier Pass north to the confluence of the Blue and Swan rivers and from the Ten Mile Range east to the historic towns of Rexford and Swandyke originated in spring, 2021.

Using information taken from first-hand accounts such as the mining district logbooks from 1859 and early 1860 and newspaper articles written by those who had observed and reported what they saw and then personally exploring the sites, alone and with others, I mentally traveled back in time imagining life at those locations over 150 years ago. I hope readers will do the same as they read the books in this series.

The *Chasing the Dream* series told the stories of Parkville, Rexford, Swandyke, Wapiti, Valdora, and Tonopah Camp 2. This series will include abbreviated versions of their history.

As I started identifying all the historic sites within my chosen boundaries, I decided to include railroad stations, even though some of them were not truly townsites. I selected 27 sites—some relatively unknown; some known by a few. About most, little had been written.

It soon became apparent that the "book" I envisioned would exceed 1,000 pages of text, documents, and maps—and that didn't count the more than 1,050 figures/photographs I wanted to include.

After discussions with my co-author and others, I concluded that a series of books made more sense. Sandie suggested the title, *Historic Landscapes, Summit County, Colorado*. We divided the sites into two categories: ghost towns and townsites with five books; and railroad stations and sites with two books. Will we expand the boundaries of the research leading to more books? Perhaps.

Figure PR-1 includes the location of all the ghost towns, historic townsites, and train stations found in *Historic Landscapes, Summit County, Colorado*.

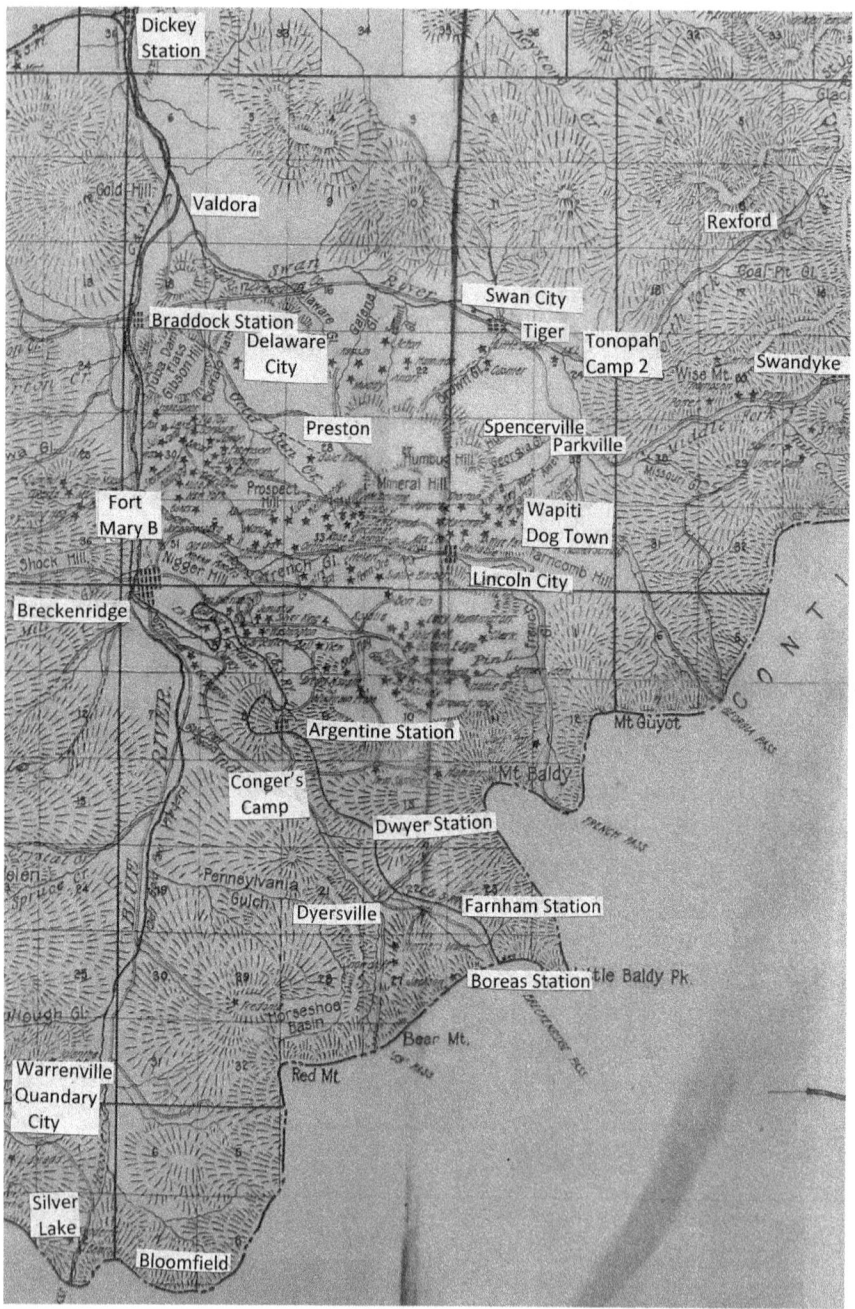

Figure PR-1. Map of a Portion of Summit County showing Ghost Towns, Historic Townsites, and Train Stations. (Author's Collection)

CHAPTER 1
BLOOMFIELD

Bloomfield Townsite Location

Where could one find Bloomfield? On the Blue River? At the head of the Blue? In Middle Park? It does not appear on any maps; no photographs exist……….

The New Town

……..but the Peruvian Mining District log book provides some information in an August 11th, 1860 entry:

J M Bloomfield }
Jms K Coath } Geo C Chamberlain
W T Richardson & Co}

For the above Company claims Twelve hundred and Eighty Acres of land for a Town Site and Ranching purpose Running one half mile East One Mile West one half mile South, and one Mile North, being one and one half miles East and West and one and one half Miles North and South Commencing at a Stake now standing near the croping of the Blue River, and situated in Peruvian Mining District. Said Town to be called Bloomfield

The above was filed for Recording Aug 13 1860
C. P Hall Recorder
F. E. Bisell Dept

Although it was most likely on the north side of Hoosier Pass in Middle Park, the exact location remains a mystery.

Two newspaper articles tell the story of the town itself; one from the September 1, 1860, edition of the *Rocky Mountain News* and the other from the September 5 edition.

In the first article, the newspaper printed the minutes of the Bloomfield Town Company stockholders meeting held on August 18, 1860, when the members elected Samuel G. Jones, president; W.T. Richardson, vice-president; D.M. Vance, secretary; and J.H. Cotes, treasurer. Members adopted a set of company bylaws. The Board of Directors included Jones, Vance, Cotes, and J.M. Bloomfield.

The company prescribed lot sizes: 50 feet in front, 140 feet deep. Blocks would measure 300 feet square. Alleys would be 20 feet wide and streets 80 feet wide. Houses must be 20 feet wide in front, 30 feet deep, 10 feet tall, and constructed with hewn timbers.

At adjournment of the meeting, D.M. Vance, secretary, signed the minutes.

The newspaper added an additional paragraph:
"Bloomfield is located on the Blue river, in the Middle Park, on the road leading from Cannon city, Fairplay and California gulch to Breckinridge. It is situated in the vicinity of fine silver, and several gold leads. The Quandary, Blacksmith or Diego, Shields, Maxwell and Live Yankee silver leads, in the immediate vicinity, are all rich. There is pine timber and water power in profusion. Several quartz leads and gulch diggings are in the vicinity; and all the appliance for arasters, quartz mills, and mining generally."

The second article on September 5 added:
"Some four or five other leads have recently been discovered in the same vicinity, which are pronounced as rich as the Quandary. Districts are being organized near the head of Blue river, almost daily, and I am informed that there is a new town laid out near the head of the Blue, called Bloomfield."

The town of Bloomfield didn't make the news again although an advertisement for Bloomfield, Ford & Co., General Commission Forwarding and Produce Merchants, appeared almost every day from September 23, 1865, until April 28, 1867, in the *Rocky Mountain News*. **(Figure 1-1)**

Other Townsite Filings

The Peruvian Mining District logbook includes three other townsite filings from 1860: August 2, Silver Ore City; August 14, Silver City; August 27, Mineral City. Although the Silver City filing states ". . . being surveyed & stocked," none of the filings resulted in a town.

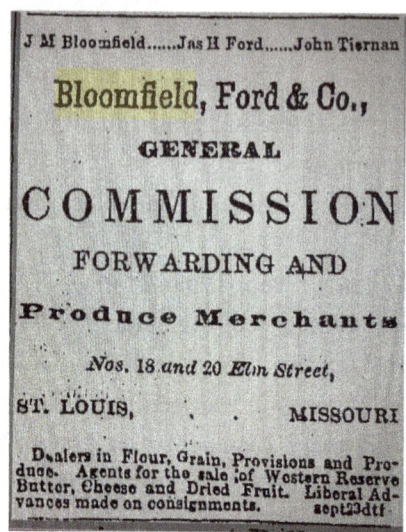

Figure 1-1. Advertisement for Bloomfield, Ford & Co., General Commission Forwarding and Produce Merchants. J.M. Bloomfield served as a member of the town's Board of Directors. (*Rocky Mountain News*, September 23, 1865)

Figure 1-2. A Mystery. Although the exact location of Bloomfield remains a mystery, the site was probably in this general area. (Google Earth, Imagery ©2021 Maxar Technologies, U.S. Geological Survey, USDA Farm Service Agency, Map data ©2021)

CHAPTER 2
SILVER LAKE

Silver Lake Townsite Location

No photographs exist of the town of Silver Lake, located northwest of Hoosier Pass. Newspapers barely mentioned it. Little is known except for its designation as a townsite in April, 1862. It had a post office, mercantile [general store], boardinghouse, and several cabins for miners.

Figure 2-1 shows Silver C, which stood for Silver City, later called Silver Lake. Other notations include Peruvian D for Peruvian Mining District; Quandary Silver L for Quandary Silver Lead; and Gibson Discovery for James W. Gibson, president of the Peruvian Mining District.

The full map (**Figure 2-2**) provides more information: "This Map is compiled from Notes of Jas. W. Gibson, who for the last two years has been engaged in exploring and prospecting this region & it is as accurate & reliable as it is possible to make it by actual surveys . . ." The map with no date but listed as 1861, predated the Peruvian Mining District, formed in April, 1862.

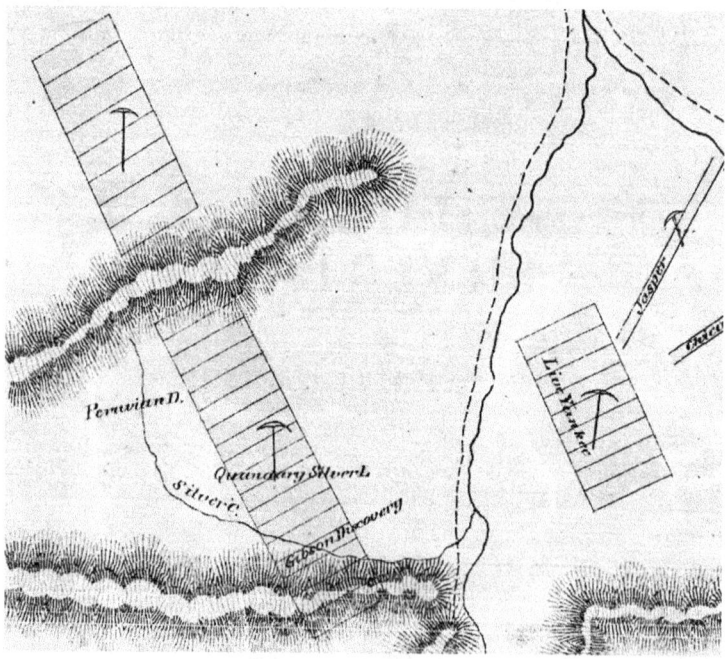

Figure 2-1. Portion of a Map showing Silver C (City), later known as Silver Lake. (Gibson Draper & Smith's Map of the Rocky Mountain Gold Regions, 1862)

Figure 2-2. Gibson Draper & Smith's Rocky Mountain Gold Regions Map, 1862.

Silver Lake Mining District

The Silver Lake Mining District came into being before the town of Silver Lake. By 1860, those prospectors arriving in South Park from Denver City found the potentially rich panning and sluicing ground "all claimed up." Using Hoosier Pass, they crossed the continental divide and headed toward the Blue River, panning as they went. They found "color" on the north side of Hoosier Pass in the upper Blue River valley.

Realizing the richness of the "upper Blue," the prospectors met a few days prior to July 16, 1860, at the camp of Enoch Welch and Company, near Silver Lake (now named Crystal Lake). Welch explained his reasons for calling the meeting:

> "That whereas rich and valuable deposit of Gold have already been discovered in Loads in this immediate vicinity and believing that further and still riches discoveries will be made here in the future. Now for the better protection of the miners here present as well as for better to develop the mineral wealth of this locality. It is proposed to submit to the sense of this meeting the propriety of the immediate organization of a mining District."

The prospectors elected Welch president and R.L. Bond recorder. They planned to reconvene at 2:00 p.m. on July 16. U.B. Fitzpatrick moved that the district would "here after be known as the Silver Lake Mining District and its boundaries shall be defined and are hereby determined as follows to-wit:

> Commencing at the trail leading from Platt River to Hoosier gulch thence northerly up the range to the head waters of the Blue and Platt Rivers – comprising all that tract of land lying between the Blue and Platt Rivers from the source thereof as far as the said 'Buckskin Joe' trail aforesaid together with the waters to the channel of either said Rivers. It being always understood that Hoosier Gulch or so much thereof as now is, or may hereafter be occupied for Gulch Mining purposes is not included in this District."

Remember that at this time, Colorado Territory had not yet been created. This area remained part of Utah Territory until February 28, 1861.

Bylaws and Claims

Those in attendance unanimously approved their bylaws, which appear as written:

"**Section 1st** The President shall until otherwise provided be the executive officer of this District. Shall hold his office for one year from the day of his election and until his successor is elected he shall be vested with the jurisdiction of a Justice of the Peace for this District. He shall call special meetings when requested so to do in writing by any actual resident of the District by causing written notices to be posted in at least three public places in the District at least giving twenty four hours notice of said meeting. He shall preside at all meetings of the District and is clothed with discretionary power to do and perform such acts and things as the welfare and best interist of the District may require of his hands.

Section 2d The Recorder shall keep a true and faithful record of all the proceedings taking place at tall the public meeting s in this District. He shall record all Claims when requested so to do and issue certificates therfor and at compensation shall receive one dollar for each as every Certificate issued by him and no more.

His term of office shall be equal as that of the President.

Sec 3d Mining Claims in this district shall be one hundred feet in length and the width of the Lode.

Sec 4th Each and Every Miner shall be intitled to hold one Claim upon each Lode as a preemption right. Also any person discovering a new Lode Shall be entitled to one hundred feet additional for his discovery Claim and any person may purchase Claims and his rights shall be respected.

Section 5th Persons taking Claims and not working the same must have them recorded immediately or they are liable to be taken and recorded by the next Claimant applaying therefor.

Sec 6th The Discovery Claim shall be the point of starting upon Lodes in this District and thence Claims shall be numbered in their order either way from Discovery. Either up and down or by specific directions as the discoverer may elect.

Sec 7th Each Miner in addition to the other Claims specified shall be entitled to one water claim by preemption of two hundred feet.

Sec 8th Claim holders shall be entitled to as many votes as they may own Claims in the District in regard to general laws and matters of interest that affect parties prorate according to the number of Claims that they may hold.

Sec 9th Until otherwise provided for parties may hold Claims without working the same until such time as they can be worked to advantage."

The claims filed in this logbook differed from those filed in any of the other Summit County logbooks transcribed by Fountain. From the very moment they created the mining district, the people filed lode claims, not placer claims. They planned to dig below ground to follow mineralized veins, not mine the surface gravels for gold.

The first time the *Rocky Mountain News* printed any information about the Silver Lake Mining District (September 3, 1860), the article affirmed the interest in lode mines: "In the Silver lake District alone, eight gold and one or two silver leads have been discovered."

The people defined, named, and registered their claims north and south or east and west of the discovery claim starting with claim number 1. Between July 4, 1860, and March 22, 1863, they filed 56 lode claims, which included 1519 individual claims and averaged 27 individual claims in each lode claim. People with multiple claims owned about 20 percent of those individual claims. Women filed 21 individual claims. Water claims totaled 53.

Lode claims could be family affairs. The claims filed on the McCoy lode, discovered July 22, 1861, included 29 individuals with a last name of McCoy. Sixteen women in the family filed claims.

Many familiar names appear in the logbook: R. [Ruben] J. Spaulding,

Chapter 2 Silver Lake

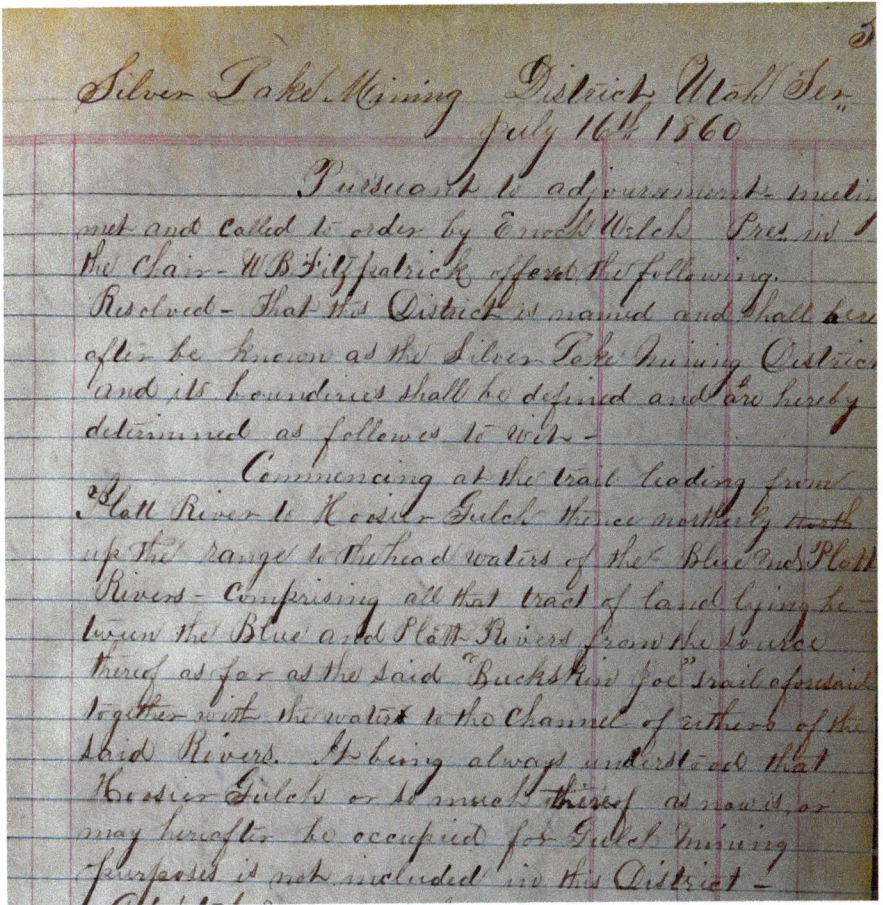

Figure 2-3. Partial Page from the Silver Lake Mining District Logbook, July 16, 1860. The logbook defined the boundaries of the mining district. Note the beautiful penmanship and dearth of spelling errors. (Photograph by Author)

leader of the group making the first recorded discovery of gold in the Blue River; Geo. Brestler [Bressler], proprietor of a livery stable on the northeast corner of Lincoln and Main in Breckenridge; M. [Marshal] Silverthorne [Silverthorn], judge of miner's court; Peter Muleback [Muhlebach], one of the first group of county commissioners; John Nolan, manager of the Sisler holdings in French Gulch after the death of John Sisler; Lelon Peabody, Wm. H. Iliff, member of the Spaulding group and owner of a very rich claim along the Blue River next to the Spaulding claim; W.P. Pollock, first county clerk and reorder; J. [John] W. Sisler, owner of a large placer mining operation in French Gulch; E. [Ezra] Stahl, Felix Pozanasky [Poznansky], person who platted an early townsite along the Blue River; and William Bemrose, discoverer of a very rich placer claim just north of Hoosier Pass.

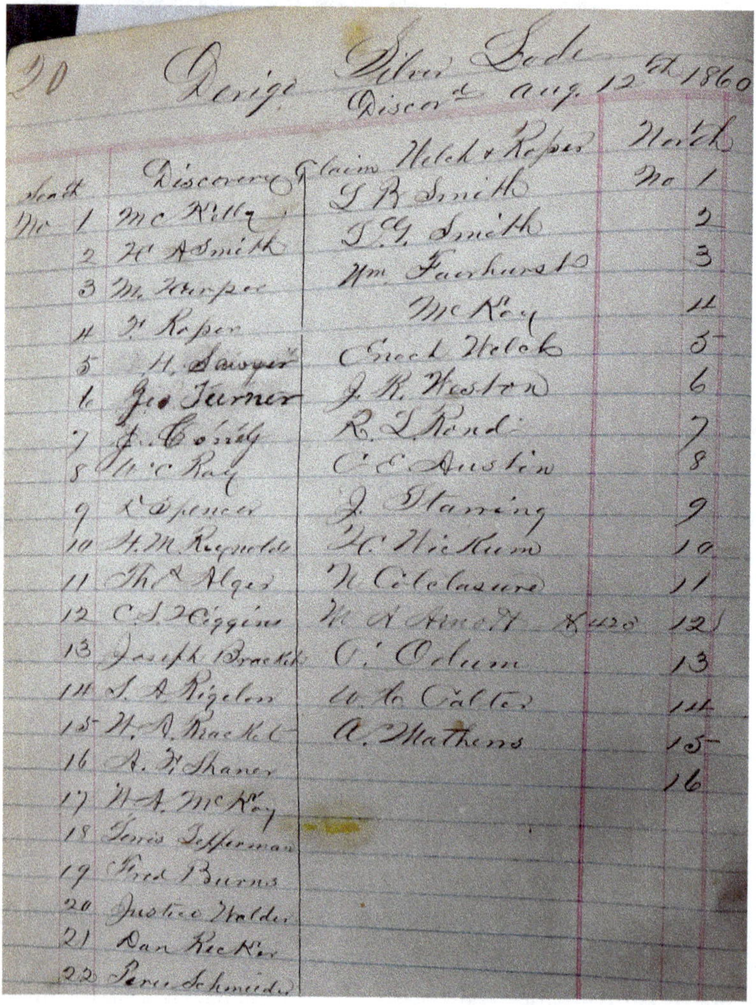

Figure 2-4. Portion of a Page from the Silver Lake Mining District Logbook showing the Derigo Silver Lode, August 12, 1860. This lode included 51 claims filed to the south and 15 claims filed to the north. R.J. Spalding (most likely Ruben Spaulding) owned claim number 3, south. (Photograph by Author)

Claim Sales

It didn't take long for some who had preempted claims to realize they could make more money by selling their claims than working them. On July 2, 1860, I.N. Buck sold his claim to J.C. Malcomb for $100; on September 13, 1860, John W. Davis sold his claim to Lafe G. Smith for $50 cash. This happened repeatedly in Summit County. Prospectors established a claim, proved its worth, and then quickly sold it.

As time passed, some claims sold for a great deal of money. On April 5, 1862, R.L. Bond sold his claim No. 1 on the Vermont lode to Henry S. Barber for $100; on July 24, 1862, H.F. Sawyer sold his No. 4 claim on the Welch lode to Wm. Dunn and David Parton for $250; on August 27, 1862, Thos. D. Burns sold his claim on the Morning Star to John Teirman and Chas. G. Northrop for $300. Prices generally increased as claims proved their worth and available placer ground decreased. On September 22, 1862, Enoch Welch sold two of his many claims to E.J. Elmer for $600 and R.H. Quinn sold his interest in seven claims for $500.

New President and Recorder

The miners of the Silver Lake Mining District scheduled their annual meeting for July 4, 1861, but unanimously decided to delay their meeting until July 8. They reconvened on that date with Enoch Welch, president, "in the chair." R.S. Bond, the recorder, did not attend. Those attending elected T.L. Mackay president and Enoch Welch recorder for the coming year.

At a subsequent meeting on July 19, 1861, the group by "Resolution" imposed an assessment of five dollars on all the claims recorded in the Derigo Silver lode for the purpose of "prospecting and defining the same." The resolution added: "a company known as the Silver Lake Mining company be allowed to take, have and to hold ten of the new forfeted claims on the Derigo Silver lode ..."

When the group met next on September 21, 1861, they selected Doc Levitt as temporary chairman because T.L. Mackay did not attend. A review of the bylaws and a discussion of any needed changes resulted in a motion allowing the bylaws to stand as written for the coming year.

The minutes in the logbook indicated some problems with miners in two mining districts (Montgomery and Morrison) on the Park County side of the continental divide filing claims on the Summit County side within the Silver Lake Mining District. The miners passed a resolution agreeing that they would not recognize those claims unless the owners filed them with the Silver Lake Mining District.

Making the News in 1861

The *Rocky Mountain News* included little about the Silver Lake Mining District in 1861:

October 26:
> "Silver Lake District is situate immediately North of Montgomery—several very rich discoveries have been made here. One gold dirt crevice was opened there some eight or ten feet in width."

December 10:
> "... During last summer some, ore prospects were made in the same mountains, by some hardy miners, among whom was Mr. Enoch Welch, who discovered the Vermont lode and several others in the Silver Lake district, situate between the head of the Platte and the head of the Blue rivers on the Snowy Range. Being attracted by those discoveries, made in the same country I had prospected a year before, I started to look for myself, and found them as rich, or somewhat richer than I expected. In company with Mr. Welch I discovered the Eugenie Lode, which bids fair to be as rich as the Vermont, when well opened. I secured claims on several lodes, but soon after the Independent, Montgomery, Pollok [should be Pollock] and Summit districts were organized, which induced me to remove to Montgomery, as being the best place for business at the foot of the range, and where loaded wagons can come in at anything of the year ...
>
> Yours respectfully,
> ALEX REY."

Miners' Meetings in 1862

On March 31, 1862, with a quorum of claim owners present for their "annual meeting," they elected J.S. Adair, Esq. president and R.L. Bond, Esq. recorder. Their current president and recorder, T.L. MacKay and Enoch Welch, did not attend as they had "left for the States." The new officers would serve for one year from the date of the meeting.

At a meeting on August 4, 1862, those present confirmed the election of J.S. Adair as president with 96 favorable votes and R.L. Bond as recorder with 91 votes in favor. The claim owners approved a motion to "attach" the Morrison Mining District to the Silver Lake Mining District with all recorded claims being recognized upon payment of the usual compensation to the Silver Lake Mining District's recorder who would, in turn, register those claims with the Summit County clerk. This solved the problem of miners crossing the continental divide from South Park and filing claims not recognized by the Silver Lake Mining District.

Before adjournment, the owners formed a committee to confer with a similar committee from the Pollock Mining District, located adjacent and north of the Silver Lake Mining District, with the purpose of uniting the two districts. Forming the committee afforded the miners the time they needed to consider the advantages and disadvantages of merging. Not until July 3, 1863, did they render their decision.

Silver City

Silver City, the town, began with an entry in the Silver Lake Mining District logbook, appearing here exactly as written:

"To all whom these presence may concern Knowye that we John S Adair Enoch Welch Gaylord G Bissell and Joshua Cressman of District No B in the county of Summit and Teritory of Colorado do hereby declair and publish as a legal notice to all the world that we have a valid Right to occupation possession and enjoyment of all and singular that tract or parsel of land not exceeding 320 acres situate lying and being in township or district No 3 in the county of Summit in the Teritory of Colorado bounded and described as follows vz

Commincing at a stake marked No (1) on the first bench of land above Silver Lake and Running in a northerly direction 80 Rods to a stake marked No 2 thence running in a North Easterly direction 320 Rods to a Stake marked No 3 thence Running in a South Easterly direction 160 Rods to a Stake marked No 4 thence in a South westerly Direction 320 Rods to a Stake marked No 5 thence in a north westerly direction 80 Rods to stake o (1) or place of beginning the same to be held as a Town site under the name of and to be designated Silver City together with all and Singular the hereditaments and appurtenances thereunto belonging or in any ways appeterning(?)

          Witness our hand and Seal

This 12 day of April A D 1862
In presence of   John S. Adair {Seal}
            Enoch Welch {Seal}
            Gaylard G Bissell {Seal}
            Joshua Cressman {Seal}

By Gaylard G Bissell atty for said Silver City town Co

 Colorado Teritory Summit County personaly appeared before me the undersigned probate judge Garlard G Bissell and acknowledged the within foregoing declaration to be the true act and deed of Said town company and for the purpose therein Stated dated at Lincoln City this 12 day of April 1862 in Summit County Colorado Teritory

          H Hill probate judge
Summit County Colorado Teritory

          R L Bond Recorder"

The founders first named the town Silver City. Entrepreneurs in the mining West often added "city" to town names to advertise the town's importance. Only later did they change the name to Silver Lake.

So, where exactly was Silver City or Silver Lake? The logbook gives clues: "Commincing at a stake marked No (1) on the first bench of land above Silver Lake." The very first sentence of the logbook records that "Pursuant to call of a number of miners, met at the Camp of E. Welch and Co., near

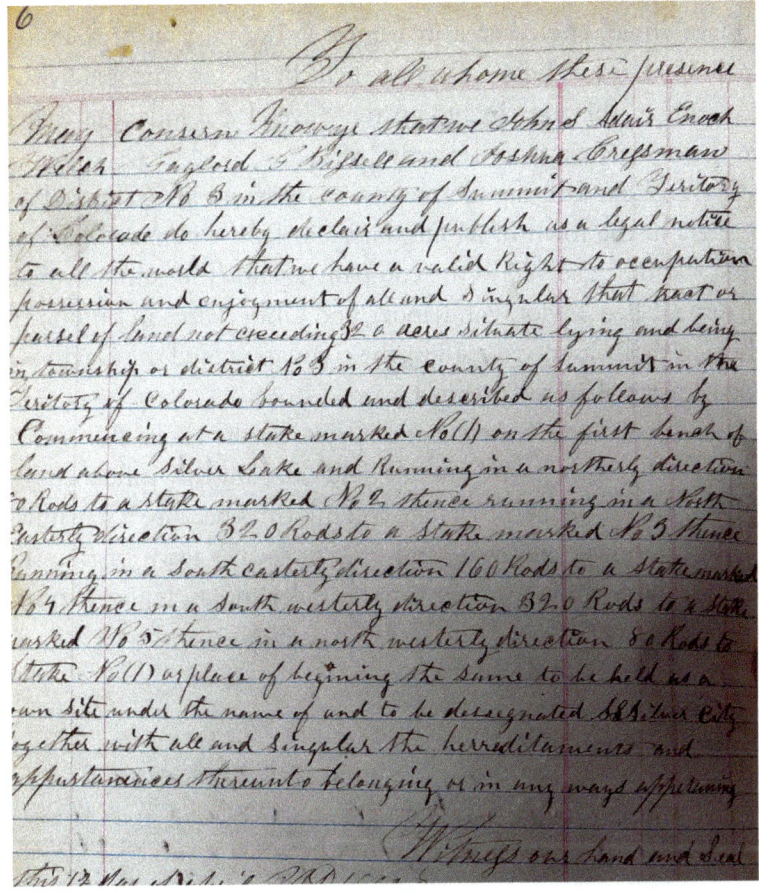

Figure 2-5. Page from Silver Lake Mining District Logbook showing the Application for a 320-Acre Townsite. (Photograph by Author)

Silver Lake so called when on motion, E. Welch was chosen chairman & L B Smith Sec. of the meeting." Water claims registered on September 6, 1861, provide another clue: "on the Streem above Silver Lake Commencing at the lower edge of the loose rock at the Foot of Welch and Morey's Slide running down the Streem."

Where, then, was Silver Lake, the body of water? The lake does not appear on any USGS maps going back to 1882; but Mineral Survey (MS) No. 527, filed on October 23, 1879, clearly shows Silver Lake as part of the Silver Lake lode. (**Figure 2-6**)

The highlighted, circled area in **Figure 2-7**, a portion of a 1940 USGS map, includes Crystal Lake. Records held by Robin Theobald, who owns several claims in this area including the Silver Lake lode and Silver Lake, confirm the name change in the early 1880s.

The Crystal Lake Mining Company, incorporated in 1879, established its headquarters in the town of Montgomery in Park County. J.J. Vandemoer, a major stockholder, served as the company agent. The company owned the Little Emma, Ellen Taylor, Vandemoer, and Ohio claims in Summit County and others in Park County. By 1880, the company added the David S. Draper and D.P. Morgan claims.

It appears that Silver Lake became Crystal Lake about this time as that name appears on maps from then on. Did the company influence the name change? Even if so, the name change still mystifies because a few miles north of the lake, at a lower elevation, and west of today's town of Blue River on Crystal Creek, one finds a Lower Crystal Lake and an Upper Crystal Lake. (**Figure 2-7**)

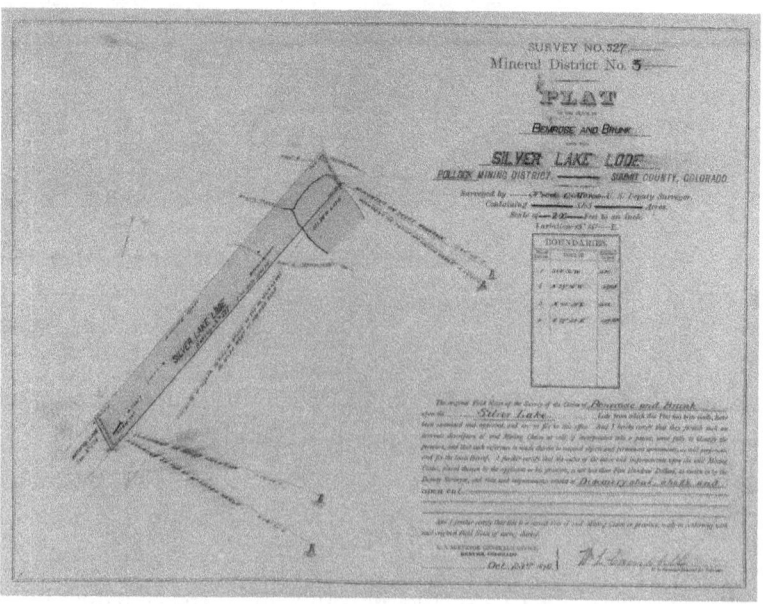

Figure 2-6. Mineral Survey (MS) No. 527, Silver Lake Lode. Bemrose and Brunk filed the survey on October 23, 1879, which clearly shows Silver Lake partially on this lode. (Courtesy Bureau of Land Management)

Chapter 2 Silver Lake

Figure 2-7. Portion of 1940 USGS Map. The black dashed line divides land in Park County (below the dashed line) from land in Summit County (above the dashed line). Hoosier Pass appears in the lower right. The highlighted yellow area includes Crystal Lake. (Author's Collection)

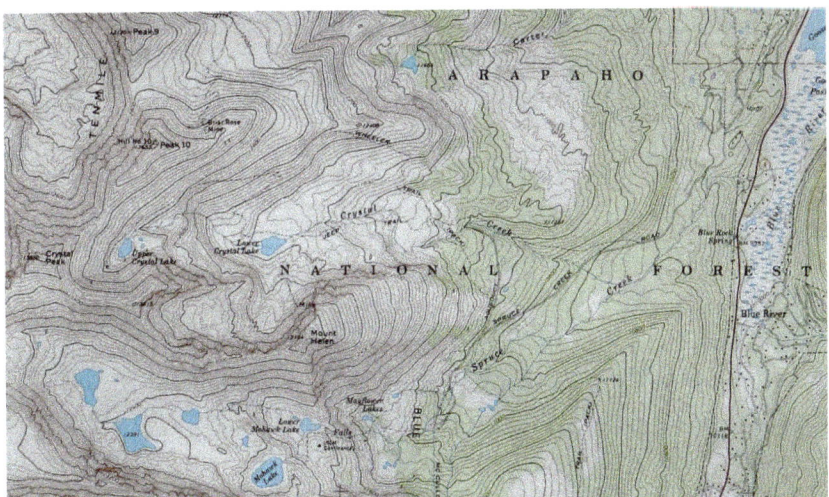

Figure 2-8. Portion of 1970 USGS Map. The map includes Lower Crystal Lake and Upper Crystal Lake, several miles north of Crystal Lake. (Author's Collection)

In the News in 1862

The *Rocky Mountain News* heralded the potential of the Silver Lake Mining District and its neighbors:

May 12:
"Pollock and Silver Lake Districts, the former within three, and the latter within two miles of here, bid fair to rival even this place, from recent discoveries. But few shafts have yet been sunk deeper than 20 feet; still, I learn from mill men most competent to judge, that the quality of the iron pyrites struck at that depth is far superior to that obtained in Gregory at a depth of 150 feet."

June 23:
"In Silver Lake district, which is just over the range from Montgomery, and at a still greater elevation, the snow has so far melted as to admit of work on several of the lodes, which is being prosecuted vigorously..."

July 8:
"...Pollock district is also spoken of with great expectations for the future. Silver Lake district is in full blast..."

August 6:
"SILVER LAKE DISTRICT
On July 25 I paid a visit to this celebrated district, which is now attracting the public notice. Messrs. Smith, Welsh and Bond were the original discoverers. The district was first organized July 4th, 1860. Up to the present date forty-two lodes have been discovered and recorded. The richest lodes are the North Star, Welsh, Welsh & Odum, Vermont, Pocahontas, etc.

A cord of top quartz from the North Star [Lode] lately yielded $292.

I went to the discovery on the Vermont [lode], across a snow field about 500 feet in width, and was much surprised at the situation of the lode—some fifteen hundred feet above the valley below. They have constructed a chute, some 1500 feet long to the valley, from which a track is laid to the water's edge, over which the quartz and crevice dirt is transported in cars.

The dirt crevice on this lode is from twenty-five to thirty feet in width. It has prospected $2.65 to the pan.

The different lodes are said to prospect finely. A wagon road is now completed from Montgomery to the North Star, and will soon be extended to the others, and the quartz will be hauled to Montgomery and crushed there, so that we will soon be in possession of astonishing results. The lodes are located on the cone of a lofty mountain, whose sides are white with the snows of last winter.

The district looks most encouraging, and in a few weeks, I expect to hear great tidings in regard to some of the lodes. Shall drop you a few lines from Buckskin Joe and vicinity.   PUNEVER."

September 4 (*Weekly Commonwealth*):
"... Leaving Montgomery, I ascended the Range, passing through Silver Lake District, and as I gained the summit, paused to look upon the beautiful scene spread out like a map away below me, and realized the rapidity with which Yankee enterprise was developing this truly wonderful country. Where, a little more than a year ago, (save the occasional crack of the hunter's rifle, the sighing or roaring of the wind, the gurgling of the Platte over the rocks, or the noises of the inhabitants of forests,) a silence prevailed which could almost be felt, now the faint hum of voices, the rolling of wagons, the noise of many hammers, the clang of machinery, the pounding of the quartz mills, and the echoing thunder of blasting fall pleasantly upon the ear.

I commenced the descent to the Blue River through Hoosier Gulch. The valley of the Blue pleased me much less than some others I had seen. The bottom, on both sides of the river, if I may call it such, is very marshy, and covered with a dense growth of brush, which renders it almost impossible to cross from one side of the valley to the other, still there is, in many places near the mountain sides, much good land and an abundance of fine timber. Excepting a few ranches, there are no settlements from Hoosier Gulch to Breckenridge ...

Yours, &c.,
HANS JACOBUS."

An Article of Agreement

The mining district's recorder entered an interesting "Article of Agreement" between C.H. Hughes and Susan Perkins [parties of the first part] and Felix Poznansky and Wm. Miller [parties of the second part] in the Silver Lake Mining District's logbook on August 10, 1862:

"Partys of first part agree to put up a Arastra upon the Claim Known as No (1) one Below on Honey Comb Lode Silver Lake Dist for and in Consideration that Partys of second Part shall pay one half of the Expenses for building the same on half in labor and the other half in money to be paid as needed. Partys of Second part shall be entitled to one half interest in the same Arastra with all the privlide of Partys of first part and it is for this agreed that Mrs Susan Perkins Party of the first Part gives unto the above company Claim No (2) two South West from Discovery on the Honey Comb Lode Silver lake District for the Benfett of the Company to be sold or to be work on equally divided between the above Company on condition however that Partys of first part shall have choice of ends."

Building an arastra, a primitive mill for grinding and pulverizing ore, in a field near a mine saved the expense of hauling heavy ore to a mill. Dr. Clinton H Scott photographed the arastra in **Figure 2-9**. An amateur photographer, Scott maintained homes in Breckenridge and in Fairplay, Park County. Thus, he repeatedly crossed the continental divide using Hoosier Pass, located in the Silver Lake Mining District. The arastra he photographed could very well be the one referenced in the logbook. Above tree line, wood rots one-tenth as fast as it would at sea level. If this arastra had been built in 1862, it would have been 37 years old in 1899 and experienced very little decay in those few decades.

Figure 2-9. An Arastra photographed by Dr. Clinton H Scott, circa 1899. (Courtesy Ed and Nancy Bathke Collection)

A Post Office for Silver Lake

To get their all-important mail from "home," those living in the Silver Lake Mining District traveled to Breckenridge in Summit County or to either Fair Play or Montgomery in Park County for those precious letters. Fair Play opened its post office on August 7, 1861; Montgomery's post office opened on July 21, 1862. Whichever way they chose, it took a good part of a day for a round trip—far too long to be away from their claims. Residents gratefully welcomed the new post office on November 22, 1862, with R.L. Bond as postmaster. It served the town until January 15, 1864.

Fairplay in South Park changed names often since its founding in 1859. Fairplay Diggings replaced the original Fair Play for a short period of time. In 1861, Platte City replaced Fairplay Diggings. The name Fairplay returned until 1869 when the town officially switched to South Park City. In 1874, townsfolk restored the name Fairplay. Virginia McConnell outlined the changes in her 1966 book, *Bayou Salado, the Story of South Park*.

D.J. Chuck's Claims

Colorado laws provided for veterans mining in the territory as this logbook entry for March 22, 1863, affirms:

"D. J. Chuck owner of Mining claims No (2) North East on the Extension of the Ruff Lode one fourth of the Discovery to the Same No (3) South West on the Maine Lode also No (2) South West on the Gold Lode to be held as Soldiers Rights agreeable to Statute Laws of Colorado he being a Soldier in Capt Wilson Company of Sharp Shooters third regiment of Colorado volunteers

R L Bond Rec"

Consolidation

At their August 4, 1862, meeting, the miners in the Silver Lake Mining District had formed a committee to explore uniting the Silver Lake Mining District with the Pollock Mining District. The miners of both districts met on July 3, 1863, at 3:00 p.m. in the town of Silver Lake to discuss the proposal further. The discussion lasted several hours. Three days later, the group met and approved a motion to consolidate. The combined district would be called the Silver Lake Mining District.

On July 11, 1863, the miners received a report from a committee appointed to consider the bylaws for the new district. The minutes noted: "Moved and seconded that the old Laws be adapted, carried"

General Election

The Summit County Commissioners on August 1, 1863, selected the home of R.L. Bond as the polling place for the upcoming general election in Precinct

No. 6. District No. 3 at Silver Lake. They chose G. Pollack, R. Spaulding, and G.H. Hughes as Judges of Election for the district.

Another Name Change

A year later the name of the combined district changed. At the annual meeting of the Silver Lake Mining District on June 20, 1864, C. McCollough moved that the name "shall hereafter be known as the Pollock Mining District." The motion carried.

As with many names written in logbooks and reported in newspapers, the spelling varied widely—sometimes within the same paragraph. For example, Pollock sometimes appeared as Pollok or Pollack.

The Last Days of the Pollock Mining District

The miners elected L. Fay president and C. McCollough recorder following the renaming of the mining district. Thus ended the entries in the Pollock Mining District logbook. Miners possibly left for new strikes or perhaps didn't return the following spring. The Pollock Mining District appears on the old Summit County mining district maps, but not the Silver Lake Mining District. (**Figure I-7**)

1872 National Mining Law

Little appears in print about mining activity in the Pollock Mining District from then until the late 1870s. The General Mining Act, passed in 1872, required anybody who had or had not filed a claim previously and wanted to continue working that claim to file with the federal government. A miner had to present a survey of the claim and pay the requisite fees before the government issued a Mineral Survey or MS number.

Second Boom in the Pollock Mining District

Hard rock (underground) mining began in earnest in Summit County in the late 1870s. The arrival of the Denver, South Park & Pacific in 1882 fostered the boom in lode mining. Now miners could bring in the heavy equipment needed for lode mining and ship ore to the mills and smelters at a more reasonable cost.

As a result of the 1872 mining law requiring owners to refile, the government issued several Mineral Surveys for the Pollack Mining District:

1879
MS526 Pacific Lode, Bemrose & Brunk
MS527 Silver Lake Lode, Benrose & Bunch

1880
MS714 Scott Lode, G.O. Scott et al.
MS715 Jason Lode, G.O. Scott et al.

1881
MS1899 Centennial Lode, The Liverpool Gold & Silver Mining Co.
MS1963 Maid of the Mist Lode, James L. Welch
MS2656B Silver Lake Millsite (unknown)
MS2627 D.P. Morgan Lode, The Crystal Lake Gold and Silver Mining and Milling Co.
MS2628 Little Emma Lode, The Crystal Lake Gold and Silver Mining and Milling Co.
MS2629 David S. Draper Lode, The Crystal Lake Gold and Silver Mining & Milling Co.

Figure 2-10. Corner Stone No. 4, (MS) No. 1713. Lode mining claims measured 150 feet by 1,500 feet. The surveyor placed a stone at each of the four corners with the mineral survey number and corner number chiseled into the rock. The numerals 7 and 1 are visible below the numeral 4. This mineral survey number does not appear on Bureau of Land Management records, indicating that this unpatented claim, located in the residential area of Silver Lake, would have been surveyed in 1881. (Photograph by Author)

The Crystal Lake Mining Company

The Crystal Lake Mining Company, incorporated in 1879 and perhaps responsible for the renaming of Silver Lake, advised the *Fairplay Flume* (February 19, 1880) that it intended to begin working their four claims (the Vandemoer, David S. Draper, Little Emma, and D.P. Morgan) quite extensively "as soon as the spring weather commences."

A follow-up article in the *Leadville Daily Herald* (February 17, 1883) revealed their plans to build a stamp mill "of the best pattern." The equipment would "arrive about the first of April. The boiler, a large, fine one, has already been taken up within one mile of the mill site at the lake on the summit of Hoosier pass." John E. Devlin, a principal of the company and their local manager, completed the experimental mill by August, 1883. No reports about the use of the mill could be found.

A few months later, the *Fairplay Flume* (May 15, 1884) announced that Devlin expected to build a large stamp mill for treating ore from the company's mines on North Star Mountain, replacing the experimental mill built the previous year. By July 24, 1884, the machinery for the stamp mill had passed through Fairplay on its way to Hoosier Pass. The *Breckenridge Daily Journal* added on July 2, 1885: "The stamp mill also, on top of this mountain above timberline, owned by Mr. Devlin, will soon be running, to make another successful season's business."

As happened with many mining operations and mining companies after the initial boom, newspapers ceased carrying information about the Crystal Lake Mining Company's mines or mills in Summit or Park counties. Devlin opened an assay office in Fairplay in October, 1883. In December of 1885, the *Fairplay Flume* advised that "J.E. Devlin, assayer and manager of the Crystal Lake Mining company, has sold out his fixtures at Alma and gone east. His destination is uncertain."

Father John Dyer, who held stock in several mining companies, stated that only the directors and officers of mining companies made any money. Could this have been the situation with the Crystal Lake Mining Company?

Chapter 2 Silver Lake

Locating Silver Lake in 2021

During the summer of 2021, Fountain, Robin Theobald, and Rich Skovlin traveled to the Silver Lake area several times. With maps in hand and armed with clues from the Silver Lake Mining District logbook, they explored many hours before locating the townsite.

They found the townsite "stake No. 1" a few feet north of Silver Lake (called Crystal Lake on current maps). Using the logbook's description for "stake No. 2," they paced off 80 rods (1,320 feet) to the north. From there, again following the description in the logbook, they estimated the locations of stakes No. 3 and No. 4.

Dense thickets of willows presented problems finding the stakes and evidence of habitation. Pushing through the willows, looking for cabin footprints, refuse dumps, and artifacts proved difficult and tedious, but not impossible. The trio discovered the footprints for some of the buildings in the residential and business sections of the town and prepared the map in **Figure 2-11** based on their findings.

Figure 2-11. Map of Silver Lake. The retail and commercial area, with post office and general store, occupied the land between the lake and road. The residential area with the boardinghouse and several cabins lined the opposite side of the road. (Drawing by Author)

Figure 2-12. Probable Location of Corner No. 1, Silver Lake Townsite. (Photograph by Author)

Chapter 2 Silver Lake

Figure 2-13. Estimated Location of Corner No. 2, Silver Lake Townsite. Note the stack of rocks in lower left corner marking that location. (Photograph by Author)

Figure 2-14. Panoramic View of Silver Lake and Vicinity, with Townsite across the Lake. (Photograph by Author)

Few logs remain from the cabins. Trees at this elevation (tree line) could not be used for the cabins because of their small size. Instead, the men used larger trees brought from lower elevations. They would have dismantled the cabins and salvaged the logs rather than cut, trim, and prepare new logs.

Evidence of a boiler, stamp mill or crusher, and other milling equipment (**Figure 2-15**) remains in the retail and commercial area of the townsite. A beam, measuring 18 inches by 24 inches and 18 feet long, rests on top of a dozen ties. (**Figure 2-16**) The beam perhaps had been part of the mill that once stood at the townsite.

Thick willows surround a can dump found between a large retail store and the road. (**Figure 2-17**) The soldered side seam of the cans indicates manufacturing dates prior to 1887. Men probably discarded the cans in the early 1880s.

According to Theobald, the mine and mill, uphill and to the west of Silver Lake, operated in the 1920s and 1930s. (**Figure 2-18**) In the late 1980s, the Alma American Company leased that site as well as others in the area. Unfortunately, the rich ore occurred in scattered pockets preventing economically profitable mining.

Could these pockets of ore be mined for a profit today? Unfortunately, with the environmental laws in force, the problem of waste disposal, and the lack of a mill to process the ore, miners will not be returning to Silver Lake.

Figure 2-15. Location of the Mill Boiler. Only the rock foundation for the boiler and some beams remains. (Photograph by Author)

Figure 2-16. Huge, Milled Beam measuring 18 Inches by 24 Inches by 18 Feet. Notches in the beam held the ties on which the beam rests. The beam's use is unclear but perhaps it had a role in the milling process. (Photograph by Author)

Figure 2-17. A Large Can Dump among the Willows, circa early 1880s. (Photograph by Author)

Figure 2-18. Mine Dump overlooking the Mill. The workings date from the 1920s and 1930s. Silver Lake can be seen in the distance. (Photograph by Author)

Chapter 2 Silver Lake

Figure 2-19. Silver Lake Townsite from Above, 2021. (Photograph by Author)

Figure 2-20. Aerial Close-up of Silver Lake Townsite, 2021. The town of Silver Lake sat in the area to the right of the lake and road. Silver Lake has become Crystal Lake on present-day maps. (Google Earth, Imagery ©2021 Maxar Technologies, U.S. Geological Survey, USDA Farm Service Agency, Map data ©2021)

CHAPTER 3
QUANDARY CITY

Quandary City Townsite Location

Quandary City (sometimes spelled Quandry), found a short distance up Monte Cristo Gulch, sat in the shadows of some of the tallest peaks of the continental divide. Quandary Peak (elevation 14,268') towered over the settlement at the southern end of Summit County, near Hoosier Pass. The town, organized prior to 1882, consisted of a hotel and smelter. (**Figure 3-1**) The mine location, dated August, 1862, predated the town.

Figure 3-1. USGS 1882 Map showing Quandry [Quandary] City. Note the hotel and smelter. The narrow line at the far right of Section 1 indicates the Blue River. (Author's Collection)

An Interesting Name

Prospectors investigated the area quite early, possibly as early as the fall of 1859 after crossing the divide. They explored Monte Cristo Gulch as they panned their way along the Blue River.

How did the peak and city receive its name? The story goes something like this: A party of prospectors discovered an immense mineral body on the mountain. Believing it would provide great riches, they staked their claims and took samples to an assayer for analysis. Even though the assays didn't provide the results the prospectors wanted, they returned to their claims in the spring. After months of labor and repeated unfavorable assays, the men labeled the mineral a "quandary" and abandoned their claims in a quandary as to whether their claims would ever produce a profit. Mount Quandary took its name from the unknown mineral found on the claims. The name changed to Quandary Peak, perhaps in 1874, although an 1882 USGS map still showed the name as Mount Quandary.

The Peruvian Mining District

On August 11, 1860, about 300 miners attended a meeting near the Quandary lead (mine) with the intention of forming a new mining district. They chose the name Peruvian Mining District (Did the name reflect the dizzying elevations in the area?) and elected James W. Gibson as president, C.P. Hall as secretary and recorder, and J.E. Bissell as deputy recorder. They set their boundaries: "The Snowy Range on the Southwest and extend[ing] Northeast from their summit six miles; the line to be the Discovery Lead," meaning the district started at the ridge of Hoosier Pass and extended north of present-day Monte Cristo Gulch.

(Refer to **Figure 2-1** for the locations of the Quandary Silver Lead, Peruvian District, and Gibson Discovery.)

The recorder entered the claims in the Peruvian Mining District logbook through November, 1860, but the district does not appear on any mining district maps. Perhaps it merged with the Silver Lake Mining District when that district formed on July 16, 1860. (See **Chapter 2**.) Because the Silver Lake Mining District organized a month before the Peruvian Mining District, it would have taken precedence and absorbed the smaller district. The Silver Lake Mining District merged with the Pollock Mining District on July 3, 1863.

The Quandary Lead or Mine

The *Leadville Weekly Herald* (May 1, 1880) provided some interesting history of the early days in Monte Cristo Gulch. A "Mr. Mills" remembered that in 1860, "he took up one of the first locations made there and named it the Quandary." A search of the Pollock Mining District logbook confirms that a miner named "Mills" actually registered 22 claims in October, 1861. Unfortunately, the records didn't provide a first name for Mr. Mills. He explained that the miners did little work on their claims until 1866 when McCollough and Gargeaut opened their smelter. Not long after, the owners experienced difficulties processing the ore. Losing money, they abandoned the smelter after one season.

Quandary City

Book A, found in the Summit County Clerk and Recorder's Office, records the Quandary City Company's filing for a townsite on August 6, 1862. Filers included Ble Brooks, Canada McCollough, Silas Brown, and George W. Lechner, some of the earliest miners in the area.

Between 1861 and 1863, the same four men, Brooks, McCollough, Lechner, and Brown, filed well over 100 claims in the Pollock Mining District. Others from the McCollough family filing claims included A.D. McCollough, S.O. McCollough, J.G. McCollough, M.H. McCollough, and E.A. McCollough.

On August 9, 1862, Ble Brooks became president of the Pollock Mining District with Canada McCollough recorder in 1862 and early 1863 when Silas Brown replaced him.

An entry on August 16, 1862, in the Pollock Mining District logbook offered details on a tunnel:

> "Know all men by these presents That We Geo W. Lechner Neah Breed and Ble Brooks have this day located a Tunnel site near the & foot of the Quandary Mountain and the forks of Silver creek and branch thereof, commending at a stake in the mouth of said Tunnel. Thence mining Westerly up the mountain 2000 ft, said claim embracing 200 ft on each side of main Tunnel Known by the name of the Keystone Tunnel and taken according to a Low of the Territory, regulating Tunnel claims"

Chapter 3 Quandary City

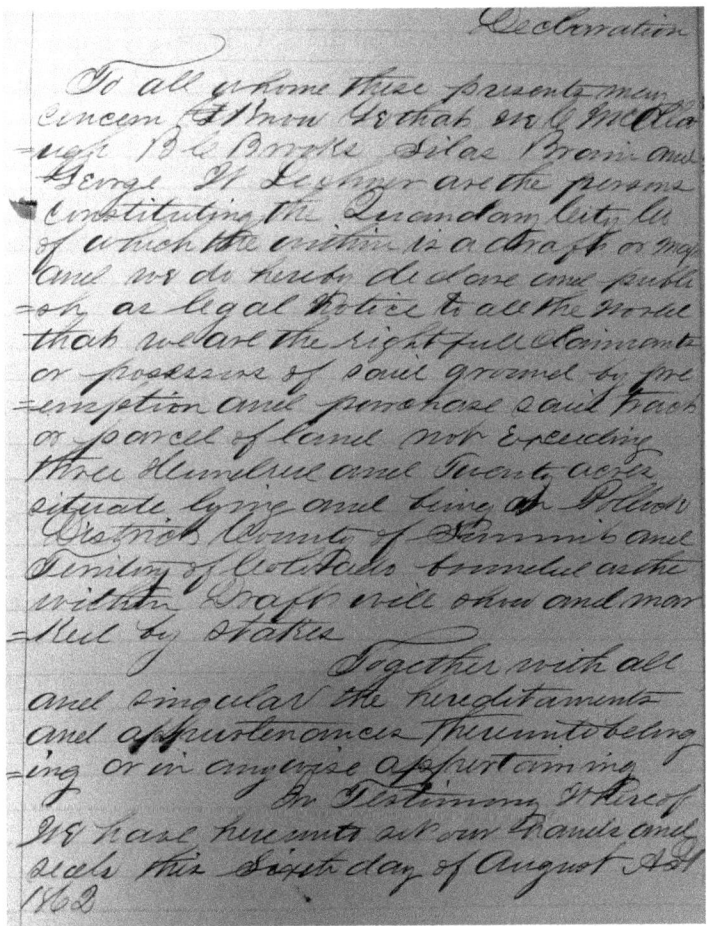

Figure 3-2. Application for the 320-Acre Quandary City Townsite in Book A by Brooks, McCollough, Brown, and Lechner on August 6, 1862. (Courtesy Summit County Clerk and Recorder's Office)

The El Dorado Mill

On the opposite side of Monte Cristo Gulch from Quandary City sat the El Dorado mill. **(Figure 3-3)** The large mill, mistakenly called the Senator mill by some, and the Quandary City hotel can be seen on the far right. Nothing remains of the true Senator mill, which had been located about a half mile west of the El Dorado mill.

Because the mill does not appear on the USGS map in **Figure 3-1**, the mill must have been built after 1882. *The Carbonate Chronicle* on April 18, 1885, welcomed the plan to build the mill:

"The *Breckenridge Leader* is authority for the statement that a twenty-stamp mill is to be erected at Quandary City on the Blue. If this be true it will be received with pleasure by a number of miners in this camp who own claims in that section."

Eric Twitty provided background on the builders:

"Prospectors William King and Joseph Rankin encountered pockets of gold and silver ore in a limestone ledge and claimed the formation as the Eldorado in 1879. They patented the property at once but did little with the find beyond shallow development work, and then sold it to W.H. and M.M. Howe within several years. Howes were Pennsylvania investors who were interested in the Hoosier Pass area, and they owned several other prospects. These other properties apparently consumed the Howes' attention, because they developed the Eldorado only to a minor degree during the early 1880s and suspended further work."

The Monte Cristo mine, located north of the El Dorado mill, supplied ore for the mill to process.

Over the years, the mine and mill operated intermittently from the 1890s to the 1920s under a variety of owners.

Chapter 3 Quandary City

Figure 3-3. The El Dorado Mill in Monte Cristo Gulch, date unknown. Usually, trammers emptied their ore cars into the top floor on the uphill side of a mill. Machinery and chemical processes reduced the size of the pieces and eliminated much of the waste rock as the ore dropped to each successive lower level. Here, the ore had to be lifted to the upper floor before processing. The hotel in Quandary City can be seen on the far right. (Courtesy Maureen Nicholls)

Figure 3-4. The El Dorado Mill, 1953. (Western History Department, Denver Public Library, X-3576)

Figure 3-5. Tram at the El Dorado Mill, 1953. The tram carried ore from the mine to the mill. (Western History Department, Denver Public Library, X-3565)

Chapter 3 Quandary City

A Name Change

In 1880, newspapers followed the action at the Monte Cristo (Christo) mine, confirming the name change from Quandary to Monte Christo mine. With Dr. C.E. Warren (See **Chapter 5**.) as one of the principal investors, the Monte Cristo Mining Company constructed buildings and purchased machinery to develop the mine. A May 11, 1880, article in the *Rocky Mountain News* prepared by Arthur Lakes, a well-known professor at the School of Mines in Golden, Colorado, repeated the name change in the headlines: "**QUANDARY, ALIAS MONTE CRISTO MINE.**" The author added: "I rode up the park to examine the Quandary mine, since become better known as the Monte Cristo." Numerous references confirmed the change.

The 1940 USGS map in **Figure 3-6** shows the locational relationship between Monte Cristo (Quandary) mine and the El Dorado mill; the mine stood north of Quandary City and the mill due south. Because Quandary City had been long gone by 1940, it doesn't appear on the map; but it would have been between the first "D" in Dorado and the double line indicating a road.

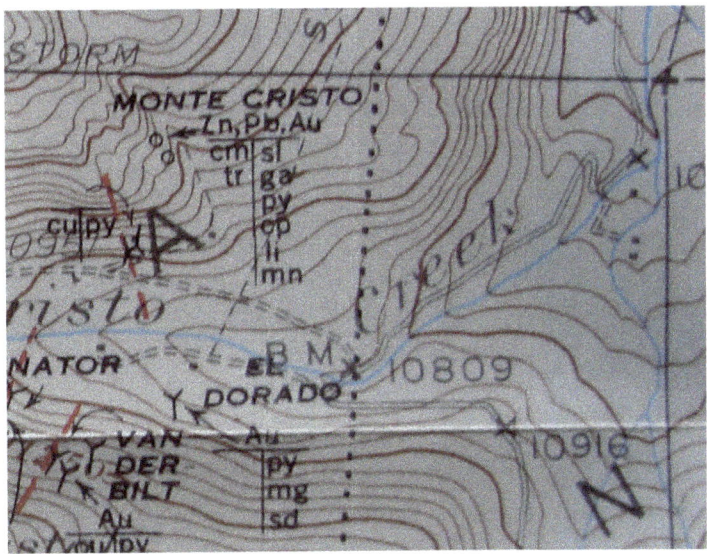

Figure 3-6. Portion of 1940 USGS Map showing the El Dorado Mill and the Monte Cristo Mine, originally the Quandary Mine. Quandary City sat between the first "D" in Dorado and the double line representing a road. (Author's Collection)

In the News

The *Leadville Daily Herald* (July 26, 1882): "Reports from Quandary City, on the Upper Blue, are favorable. New mines are being discovered and good strikes in both old and new claims are reported."

The *Alma Bulletin* (February, 1882): "A seventy-horse power engine at the new concentrating works at London Junction, Colorado came from the Monte Cristo mill at Quandary City."

The *Montezuma Millrun* (July 21, 1883): Joe Prest fatally [shot] Elmer C. Smith at the Lackwana mine "located a mile above Quandary City."

The *Breckenridge Leader* (April, 1885): "A twenty-stamp mill is to be erected at Quandary City on the Blue. If this be true it will be received with pleasure by a number of miners in this camp who own claims in that section."

The Last Reference

(Undated): "The ghost town of Quandary City on North Star Mountain was home to mine owners who were seeking quartz carrying gold, silver and copper ores."

Quandary City in 1953 and 1975

Muriel Wolle visited Monte Cristo Gulch in 1953 and photographed the El Dorado mill and the still-standing hotel in Quandary City. (**Figures 3-4, 3-5, 3-7**) Perhaps squatters had preserved the hotel by replacing or repairing the original roof.

In 1975, John Daugherty, while documenting the El Dorado mill, included the hotel in his photographs. (**Figure 3-8**) Still standing but showing increased roof deterioration, it wouldn't be long before it collapsed.

Chapter 3 Quandary City

Figure 3-7. The Hotel at Quandary City, 1953. (Western History Department, Denver Public Library, X-3566)

Figure 3-8. The 1882 Quandary City Hotel, 1975. The remains of the El Dorado mill can be seen on the right in the background. (Courtesy of the Summit Historical Society)

2021

In the summer of 2021, Fountain revisited the Quandary City townsite with Robin Theobald, Rich Skovlin, and Rick Hague. Although the walls had collapsed, some logs on each side remained standing. (**Figures 3-11** and **3-12**) They drew the map in **Figure 3-10**.

The log hotel, one and one-half stories high, measured 30 feet by 15 feet. A living room and kitchen filled the lower level; guests slept on the upper level. (**Figure 3-10**) Logs with dowels in the ends connected to the ends of logs in the adjoining walls for additional support. Large metal spikes at the corners provided even more support for the walls. (**Figure 3-13**) Both square (cut) and round (wire) nails had been used in constructing and maintaining the structure, indicating that people had occupied the building for many years.

The group found a wooden trunk from the 1880s in the back of the collapsed hotel. Although much of the wood had rotted, the rusted hardware remained in place. A small square box found inside the trunk would have held valuables.

In front of the cabin, several large rocks had round drill holes and a few triangular starter holes in them. Pneumatic drills created the round holes while hand steels created the triangular holes. Because these rocks contained no ore, it can be assumed that the holes resulted from a drilling contest of some sort.

Workers built the hotel on a raised area above the Monte Crisco Creek. (**Figure 3-10**) People walked about 25 feet from the hotel to "answer the call of nature."

They chose a spot east of the cabin and north of the Monte Cristo Creek for the smelter. (**Figure 3-1**) A water wheel or possibly a Pelton wheel brought water from the creek to a flume that led to a coke-burning furnace. Bellows increased the temperature of the smoldering coke, which in turn helped extract the gold and silver.

The blacksmith shop, which stood next to the furnace and downhill from the hotel, contained a forge. Note the slanted roof in **Figure 3-7**. On the opposite side of the creek, a cabin held supplies for the smelter.

Chapter 3 Quandary City

Figure 3-9. The Location of Quandary City, 2021. The remains of the hotel can be seen on the right with the crumbling remains of the El Dorado mill in the distance to the left. (Photograph by Author)

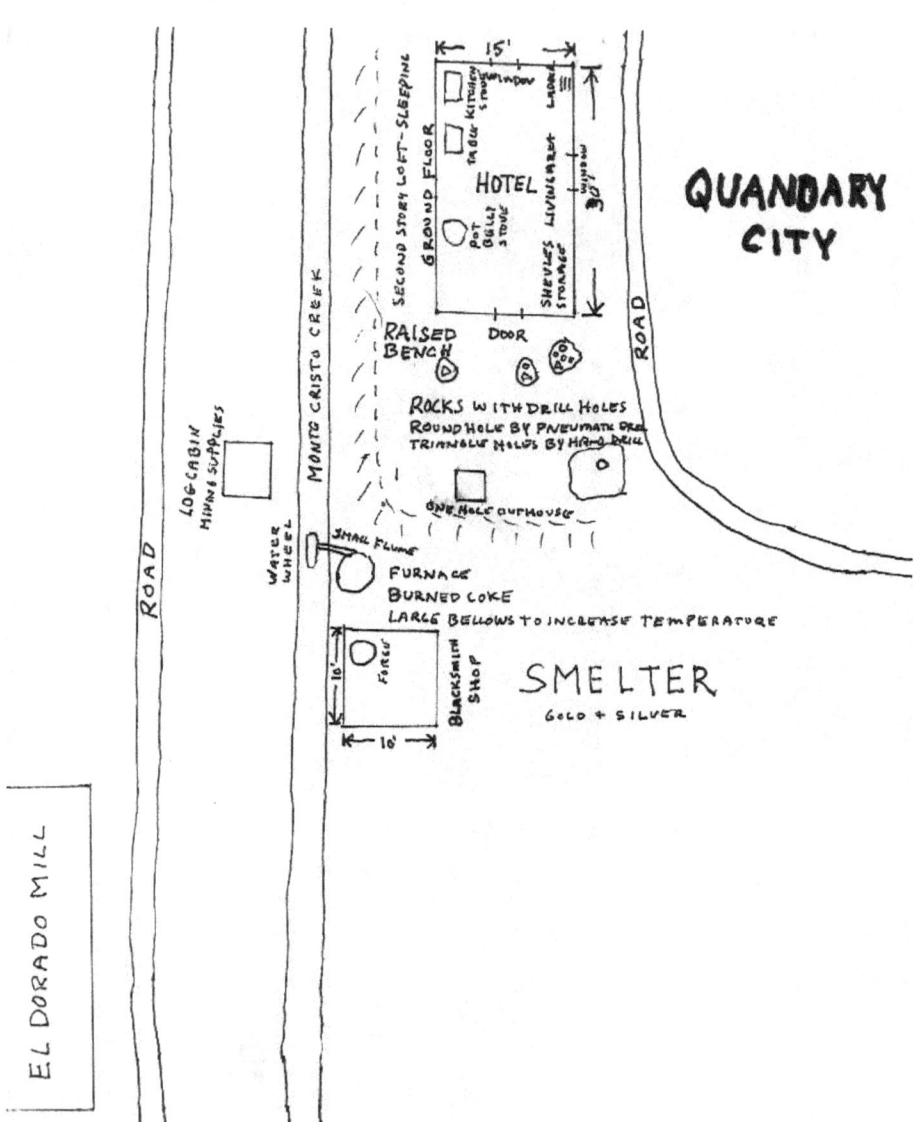

Figure 3-10. Hand-drawn Map of Quandary City. Fountain and Skovlin based the map on evidence found at the site. (By Bill Fountain and Rich Skovlin)

Chapter 3 Quandary City

Figure 3-11. Quandary City Hotel from the Front, looking West. (Photograph by Author)

Figure 3-12. Quandary City Hotel from the Back, looking East. (Photograph by Author)

Figure 3-13. Dowels to Secure Overlapping Logs. The dowels and large square metal rods provided extra strength to the hotel's walls. (Photograph by Author)

Figure 3-14. A Trunk from the 1880s. Found at the back of the hotel, the wooden trunk had rotted but the metal hardware and a small, inner box for valuables remained. (Photograph by Author)

Chapter 3 Quandary City

Figure 3-15. One of Several Large Rocks with Drill Holes in Front of the Hotel. (Photograph by Author)

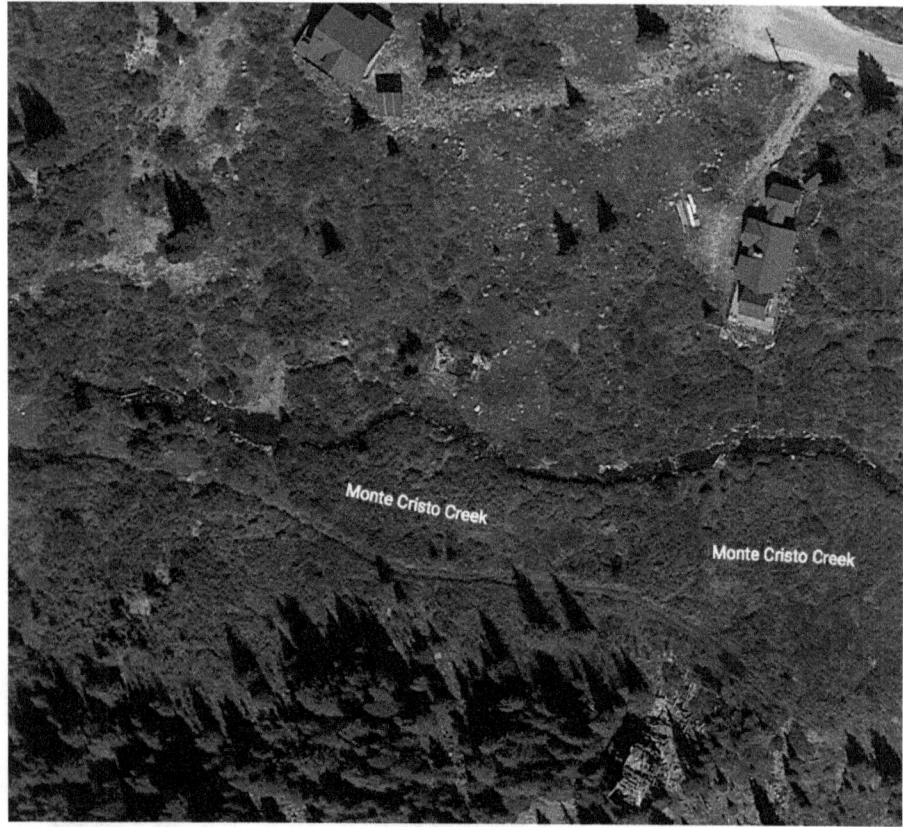

Figure 3-16. Aerial View of Quandary City Townsite in Monte Cristo Gulch. Remnants of the hotel in Quandary City can be seen in the center of the photograph with the El Dorado mill to the lower left. (Google Earth, Imagery ©2021 Maxar Technologies, U.S. Geological Survey, USDA Farm Service Agency, Map data ©2021)

CHAPTER 4
CONGER'S CAMP/ARGENTINE

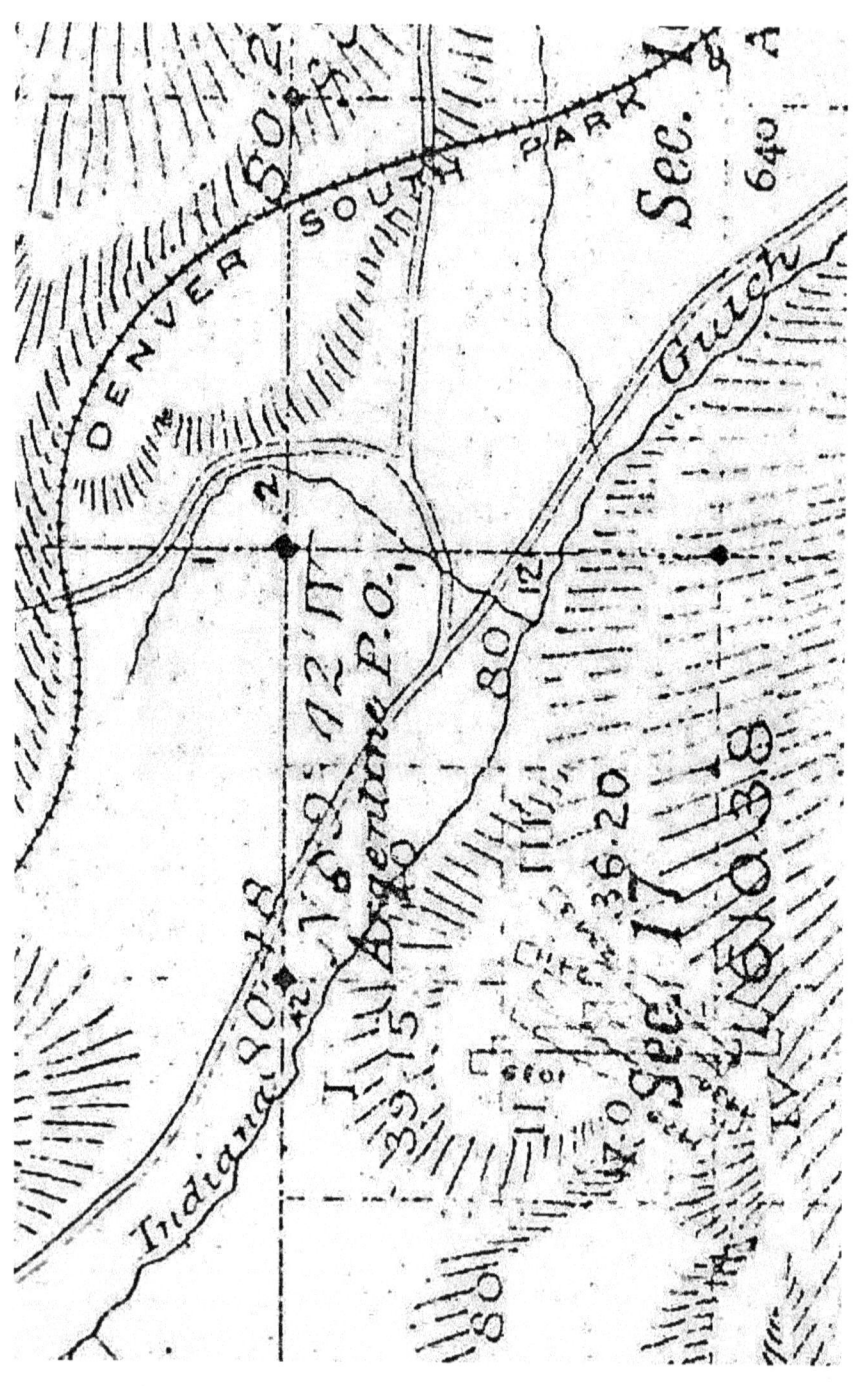

Figure 4-1. USGS 1882 Map showing Argentine P.O. (Post Office) in Indiana Gulch. Note the Denver, South Park & Pacific track on the hill. (Author's Collection)

Conger's Camp/Argentine Townsite Location

Although no known photographs of Conger's Camp/Argentine exist, its location is known—exactly: in Indiana Gulch, on the south side of Indiana Creek, today on a vacant lot in Spruce Valley Ranch. Called Conger's Camp in early 1880, the name changed to Argentine on January 3, 1881. The camp boasted several retail stores, a stage office, post office, blacksmith shop, boardinghouse, a large sawmill, and the ubiquitous saloons.

Confusion

Several books identify the location of Conger's Camp/Argentine incorrectly, most likely because Summit County had no less than three camps named Argentine; this one, dating from 1881, being the oldest.

A second "Argentine," located on Peru Creek, began life as Decatur, founded in 1868 by "Commodore" Stephen Decatur Bross. It received a post office on October 3, 1879, but when the mines failed, the post office closed on January 28, 1885. New discoveries of gold, copper, and lead rejuvenated the mines, the town grew and again merited a post office. Federal postal regulations at the time stipulated that when an abandoned post office reopens, it must be under a new name. Using the name Rathborne, the post office reopened on September 19, 1891.

A few years later, the cycle repeated itself: boom turned to bust—the mines closed—merchants moved away. When new discoveries in 1901 caused a resurgence, the post office reopened, this time taking the name Argentine because of the camp's proximity to Argentine Peak (elevation 13,738') and Argentine Pass (elevation 13,207'). When the boom faded, the post office closed on February 28, 1907.

Not a town at all, the third "Argentine" functioned as a Denver, South Park & Pacific station between Boreas Pass and Breckenridge. This location, due north and up the hill three quarters of a mile from Conger's Camp/Argentine, caused the confusion.

The portion of the colored map in **Figure 4-2** comes from a large map entitled "Topographical Map of the Blue River Gold Fields and Metal Mines, Summit County, Colorado" by F.C. Cramer. Small squares inside a large

Figure 4-2. Portion of 1900 Colored Map by F.C. Cramer. The map incorrectly shows Argentine as a town on the Denver, South Park & Pacific "High Line," rather than simply a rail station. The name of the station changed to Bacon in 1906. Many have mistakenly taken this location as the site of Conger's Camp/Argentine. (Author's Collection)

square portray Argentine as a town, instead of a railroad station with station house, ore bin, and platform for loading ore cars parked on the siding. Workers laid the track there in 1882. Cramer drew a similar, but black and white, map in 1906 entitled "Topographical Map Showing the Metal Mines of Summit County, Colorado" that used the same small square inside a larger square for Argentine.

In 1906, the railroad renamed their station Bacon. Conger's Camp/Argentine in Indiana Gulch had been abandoned by that time for many years. Because of the wide-spread use of both of Cramer's maps, authors and researchers mistakenly assumed that Conger's Camp/Argentine sat along the rail line between Boreas Pass and Breckenridge.

Samuel Patterson Conger

Samuel Patterson Conger, the son of Benoni (1812-1890) and Catherine Patterson Conger (1811-1882), was born in Monroe, Ohio, on July 1, 1835. He married his wife, Diantha (1841-1920), in 1860.

On Monday, July 7, 1879, Conger signed the guest register at the Silverthorn Hotel in Breckenridge without adding a place of residence. Just three weeks later, on Sunday, July 27, C.T. Howard and Hiram Hill signed the register and named their residence as Congers Camp. Walter McDonald, who signed on September 15, also listed Conger's Camp as his home.

Diantha Lode

The *Rocky Mountain News* on June 3, 1880, published details of Conger's life in Summit County, his discovery of the Diantha mine, and the founding of Conger's Camp in March, 1879.

One of the early prospectors in Summit County, arriving in 1859-1860, he discovered large quantities of silver varying in size from pin heads to pieces weighing as much as three ounces in the placers lining the Blue River. Conger temporarily moved to Boulder County where he earned a fortune in the silver mines of Caribou before returning to Summit County in 1879.

Recalling his discovery of silver in the Blue River 20 years earlier, he prospected east of his prior discoveries, up Indiana Gulch, trying to locate the source of the silver. In May, 1879, he discovered the Diantha lode (variously spelled Dianthe and Dianthia), named for his wife.

By the fall of 1879, others such as J.K. Wannemaker, W.A. Rand, and Alex R. Coss opened their own mines in the area and worked them through the winter.

Camp Evolution

The camp evolved over the winter and into the spring. Seybolt, Sutton & Co. purchased the sawmill and its equipment from W.J. Kinsey of Denver. The 20-horsepower mill cut 10,000 feet of lumber per day. For this reason, sawn lumber, instead of logs, formed the walls of most buildings in Conger's Camp. Business buildings would have had false fronts, providing space for advertising.

Charles I. Hayes, formerly a professor of natural sciences in the State Agricultural College of Illinois at Champaign, opened an assay office in town. Jerry T. Krigbaum operated a general store selling mining and other supplies; his wife, Lizzie, supplied the camp with fresh eggs from her flock of hens. By June, nine buildings lined the street; residents anticipated increasing the number to as many as 30.

As the town grew, it required a rudimentary government. On June 16, 1880, residents met at the tent of A.B. Powell and appointed D.C. Stover chairman and A.B. Powell secretary. "On motion Colonel Wannemaker, C.C. Haddon, N. Kirkpatrick, G.G. Gould, Capt. McMahan and John Rasenbarger were appointed a committee to report resolutions, expressive of the sense of the residents of this camp, as to its material interests."

Besides the Dianthe, numerous mines operated nearby: the Dianthe Nos. 1, 2, 3, Big Dutchman, Equator, Bismarck, Davis, Mammoth, Homestake, Bonanza, Little Daisy, Dexter, Red Man, Dolly Varden, and Dixie. Jerry N. Hill, employed by the post office, owned a property between the Dianthe and the Blue River.

1880 U.S. Census

The 1880 U.S. census for "South Blue River Valley from Breckenridge to Continental Divide," conducted on June 16, included Conger's Camp but did not list it separately. On the second of three pages, the enumerator identified Conger as "a lode miner" and his wife, Diantha, as "Keeping House." Two boarders lived with them: D.C. Stover (64), an attorney, and J.C. Morrison (25), a grocer. Next door lived Clinton Duncan (39), a teamster, his wife, five children (ages 3 to 17), and two boarders, who worked as miners. The census included the Krigbaums and their three children, ages 4 to 9.

Chapter 4 Conger's Camp/Argentine

James Cassady (Cassidy), a 32-year-old miner, as well as his 30-year-old wife, Elizabeth, and their two children, James and Patrick, ages 1 and 4, appeared on the list. A short time later, Cassidy murdered George McKernen on Baldy Mountain in a claim jumping dispute. After a trial, in which the jury found Cassidy guilty, the judge sentenced him to life in prison in the penitentiary at Cañon City. Elizabeth, with no way to support her two children, turned to prostitution to survive. (For more on the story, consult *They weren't All Prostitutes and Gamblers*, written by Mather and published by the Summit Historical Society.)

The census included C.J. Harge, teacher; E.E. Litchfield, bookkeeper; C.Y. Litchfield, superintendent for the N.R.&B.M. Co.; Peter Walsh, blacksmith; S. Fountain, laborer; Horace Smith, teamster; Joe Wynck, carpenter; George G. Gould, lode miner; J.E. Americk, machinist; and others. Not everyone living in Conger's Camp worked in a mine.

Reporter's Description of Conger's Camp

As to be expected, the camp received a visit from a *Daily Journal* reporter, who published an interesting and detailed description of the camp on March 23, 1881:

> **"Argentine**
> In crossing the range from Como to Breckenridge, the incoming passenger's attention is directed to the little village of Argentine, formerly and widely known as Conger's Camp. It resembles more than any other in Colorado (so European travelers say) a Swiss chalet. A beautiful location, surrounded by primeval forests and overlooked by towering mountains, near whose base it nestles like an infant at its parent's knee---this is Argentine. A score or more of buildings, from the cabin of the prospector to the well-built houses of prosperous mine owners, with several business buildings and the extensive sawmills of Seybolt, Sutton & Co., comprise the town proper while at many a point on the mountain sides and in the sheltered gulches may be found bachelor parties and families industriously working out their fortunes on the lodes of the camp ..."

Conger's Camp Post Office

The federal government opened the post office on July 8, 1880, with George T. Gould postmaster. On January 3, 1881, the post office changed the name of the town to Argentine with Diantha Conger postmistress. Change came slowly: **Figure 4-3** indicates that the post office still used the name Conger on January 10, 1881.

Figure 4-3. Post Card sent from Conger's, January 10, 1881. Cancellation simply consisted of an X through the stamp with "Conger 1/10 – 81 Colo" hand-written above. (Courtesy Jerry Eggleston)

Three years later, in February, 1883, the *Daily Journal* confirmed that Diantha Conger still held the position as postmistress: "Conger's Camp ... is located on the old stage road from Breckenridge to Como, across the Breckenridge pass of the main range ... two daily mails are received and dispatched, Mrs. Diantha Conger, postmistress." After the inevitable closing occurred on October 22, 1883, people from the camp traveled to Breckenridge for their mail, although the Spottswood and McClellan Stage Line, with a depot in the camp, might have carried mail to the settlement along with people and freight in their "modern" Concord coaches.

Crofutt's Guide

Crofutt's 1881 *Grip Sack Guide to Colorado* included a description of Conger's Camp:

> The camp "is a small mining and lumbering camp, situated on the stage road between Como and Breckenridge, four miles southeast of the latter, in a forest of the finest timber. A large saw mill, store, and a few other buildings comprise the camp. There are some placer mines in the vicinity, and some lode mines, which carry ruby [silver with a deep red color] and brittle silver [cracked or easily broken silver as a consequence of corrosion and weathering], silver glance [silver with a shiny luster to its lead-gray color], copper, and black sulphurets. Assays run from, $200 all the way up to $12,000 to the ton. Several of the officials of the old Hannibal & St. Joseph railroad as well as that old pioneer, W.N. Byers of Denver, and Major Hill, of the postoffice department, are interested in the mines in this locality."

There are no known photographs of Conger's Camp/Argentine but Fountain and Rich Skovlin imagined what the town might have been and drew the map in **Figure 4-4** based on building footprints, roads, and newspaper descriptions. Note the buildings with false fronts lining the main road, the stage office, and post office. The camp had the usual saloons and two-story brothel with bedrooms upstairs and saloon on the lower level.

Perhaps the main street in Congress, San Juan County, Colorado, looked like the main street of Conger's Camp/Argentine with its false front buildings. (**Figure 4-5**)

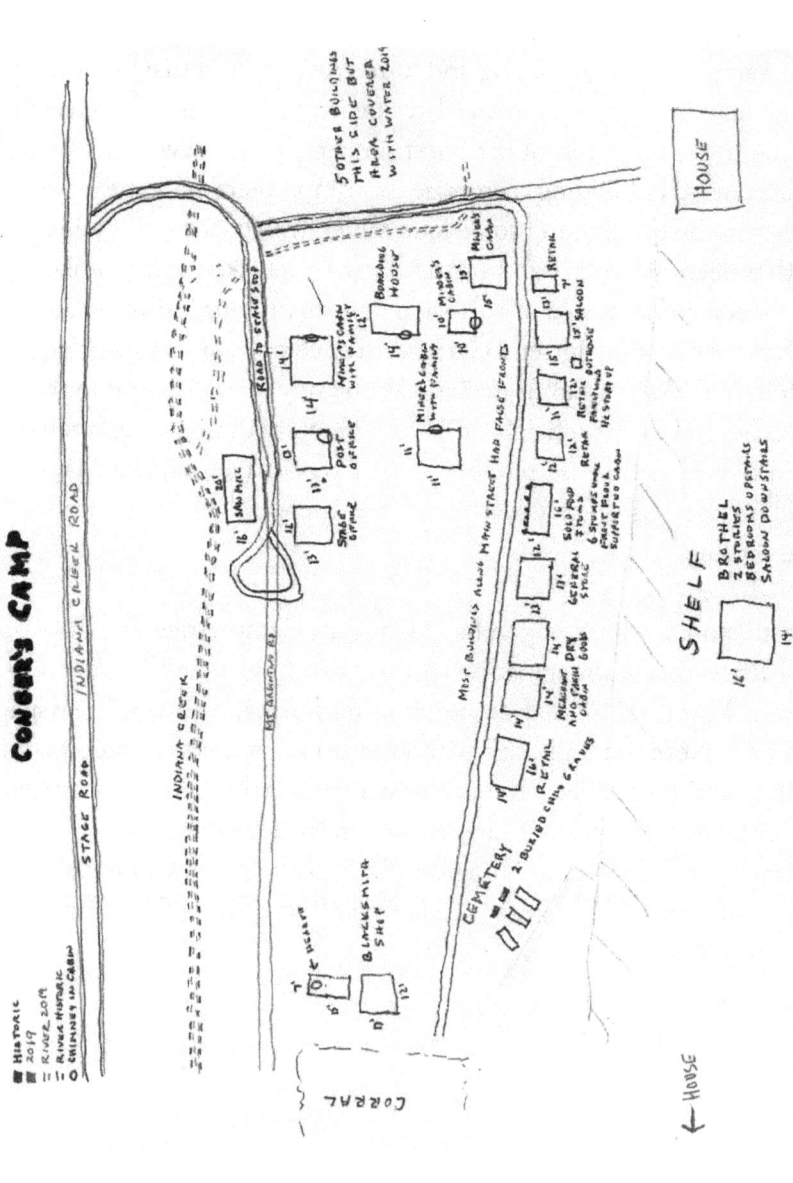

Figure 4-4. Hand-drawn Map of Conger's Camp/Argentine as imagined by Fountain and Skovlin. (Courtesy Rich Skovlin and Bill Fountain)

Figure 4-5. Congress, San Juan County, Colorado, 1880. Perhaps Conger's Camp/Argentine resembled Congress. The sloping site of Congress differed from that of Conger's Camp/Argentine, which occupied a valley floor. (Courtesy James Fountain)

Sale of the Dianthe Group of Mines

The Silver Glance Mining and Tunneling Company, incorporated under the laws of Colorado on April 2, 1881, enjoyed capital stock of $4,000,000. Denver capitalists T.M. Patterson, president, S.F. Powell, secretary, and V.D. Markham, treasurer, led the company. Conger sold or transferred ownership of the Dianthe, Dianthe Nos. 1, 2, and 3, Sam Patterson, Susan, Cottonwood Spring, Delta, and Birdie Hill lodes to the company while he took on the role of the company's "financial agent."

Not until many years later (September 11, 1890) did the company have the Dianthia, Susan, and Dianthia No. 1 group of lodes surveyed. It received Mineral Survey (MS) No. 6235 on October 20, 1890. (**Figure 4-6**) A portion of this map (**Figure 4-7**) includes the workings and cabins found on the claim at the time of the survey. Note that the spelling for the claim is now Dianthia, instead of Dianthe.

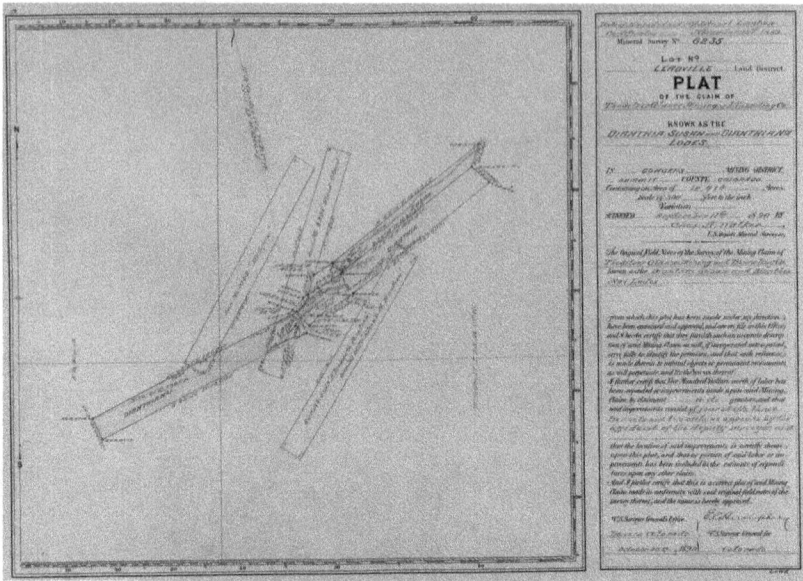

Figure 4-6. Mineral Survey (MS) No. 6235, the Dianthia, Susan, and Dianthia No. 1 Lodes, October 20, 1880. (Courtesy Bureau of Land Management)

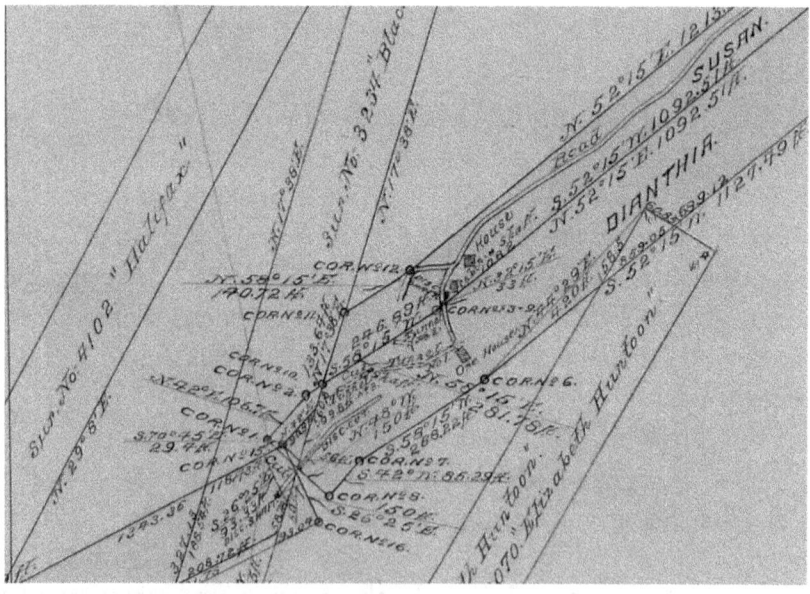

Figure 4-7. Portion of Mineral Survey (MS) 6235. Note the road, tunnels, house, and ore house. (Courtesy Bureau of Land Management)

Mining in 1883

Numerous large corporations mined the area around what was now called Argentine in 1883: The Mining Company of Hannibal, Missouri; the Lake Shore Mining Company of South Bend, Indiana; the Steadman Gulch Mining Company of Wheeling, West Virginia; the Stevens & Penfield Association of New York and Chicago; the Silver Glance Mining Company of Denver and Argentine; the High Line Prospecting and Developing Company of Denver; Thompson, More & Company of Harrodsburg, Kentucky; and various individual miners and operators.

The 1884 *Colorado State Business Directory*, using the name Conger, reported a population of 24 living along the stage line road but not enjoying the service of a post office.

The 1885 *Colorado State Business Directory*, still calling the town Conger, described it as a:

"Small mining town and lumber camp on the Como-Breckenridge road
Village set in a forest of fine timber
Four miles southeast of Breckenridge
Sawmill, a store, and a few buildings"

The *Daily Journal* (July 25, 1885) offered one last description: "Argentine that once boasted a grocery, two saloons, a beer bottling establishment, a sawmill and a local millionaire, to day has one cabin occupied temporarily by a man doing assessment work in the vicinity."

Conger's Camp/Argentine's heyday lasted three to four years, typical of a boom-to-bust mining camp. Discovery—additional claims—new town springing to life overnight—mine closures—deserted town, except for some lumbering that lasted a bit longer than mining.

Conger's Camp Today

Mark Fiester, one of the few people who found the correct location of Conger's Camp/Argentine, visited the site prior to writing his book *Blasted Beloved Breckenridge* in 1973, and described the scene: "A few scattered boards are now found in the open meadow, one finds stones outlining cabin sites.

Hardly a remnant is to be found resembling a building or cabin. Conger's Camp—Argentine—passed away almost from remembrance." He included two photographs (page 58) with the caption: "Most substantial remains of Conger's Camp-Argentine (Indiana Gulch) 1971."

Evidence of Conger's Camp/Argentine exists on one of the vacant lots in Spruce Valley Ranch, a 250-acre development started in 1977. Fortunately, surveyed lots and roads, grading and construction did not disturb the site of Conger's Camp/Argentine, except for removing buildings and trash dumps, allowing the site to be properly documented and recorded. Note that the site is on private property. **Figures 4-8** through **4-13** show the site in 2019.

Figure 4-8. Townsite of Conger's Camp/Argentine, 2019. (Photograph by Author)

Figure 4-9. Part of Main Street, Conger's Camp/Argentine, 2019. (Photograph by Author)

Figure 4-10. Location of the Stables, Conger's Camp/Argentine, 2019. (Photograph by Author)

Figure 4-11. Fireplace Rocks. (Photograph by Author)

Figure 4-12. Rock Fireplace. (Photograph by Author)

Chapter 4 Conger's Camp/Argentine

Figure 4-13. Panoramic View of the Conger's Camp/Argentine Townsite, 2021. (Photograph by Author)

Figure 4-14. Aerial Photograph showing Conger's Camp/Argentine. The town sat south of Mt. Argentine Road, extending from the driveway leading to the house on the right to the house on the left. The sawmill was on the north side of Mt. Argentine Road. (Google Earth, Imagery ©2021 Maxar Technologies, U.S. Geological Survey, USDA Farm Service Agency, Map data ©2021)

CHAPTER 5
WARRENVILLE

Warrenville Townsite Location

Reality smashed the dreams of many who planned grandiose towns in the mining West. Speculators envisioned two for Monte Crisco Gulch. Warrenville, located in 1880, near the original location of Quandary City, never saw the light of day. It does not appear on any maps and no photographs of it exist.

Townsite Plat

The Fairplay Flume on May 27, 1880, explained the town's potential:

> **"WARRENVILLE, ON THE BLUE.**
> P.O. Gaynor, the well known U.S. deputy surveyor, has been busy during the week platting the town of Warrenville on the site of the old Pollock mining district on the south fork and at the head of the Blue. The town takes its name from Dr. C.E. Warren of this city, and is about eight miles from Alma and about the same distance from Breckinridge. An old smelter that was used for treating the ores mined, when Pollock was a thriving district, has been purchased from Senator Henry M. Teller, and is being fitted out with new machinery. There are said to be many good prospects in the vicinity and some active work will be done this year. Quite a number of Alma people are prospecting there, and three Leadville companies have a force at work developing their claims. The character of the mineral shown in the mines is a free milling ore. Prospects for a lively camp there this summer are first-class."

Thus, Warrenville and Quandary City would have been neighbors. Dr. C.E. Warren, for whom the city was named, played an important role in the Monte Cristo Mining Company, which owned the Monte Cristo mine in Monte Cristo Gulch. (**See Chapter 3**.) Locating the city in the Gulch to serve the mines and their employees made economic sense. However, after the article in *The Fairplay Flume*, none of the Colorado newspapers referenced Warrenville again. The 1882 map in **Figure 3-1** shows Quandary City.

Chapter 5 Warrenville

The Fairplay Flume first wrote about Warren in their August 21, 1879, issue after he signed a one-year lease on the St. Nicholas Hotel in Alma where he planned to offer "first-class style" accommodations. Starting in February, 1880, Warren advertised "Refurnished and Refitted" rooms and bragged that "The table is Bountifully Provided."

So, count Warrenville among the towns of Summit County that probably never welcomed a resident or business.

Figure 5-1. Exact Location Unknown. Although Warrenville can't be located precisely, it would have been somewhere in this aerial image. (Google Earth, Imagery ©2021 Maxar Technologies, U.S. Geological Survey, USDA Farm Service Agency, Map data ©2021)

CHAPTER 6
DYERSVILLE

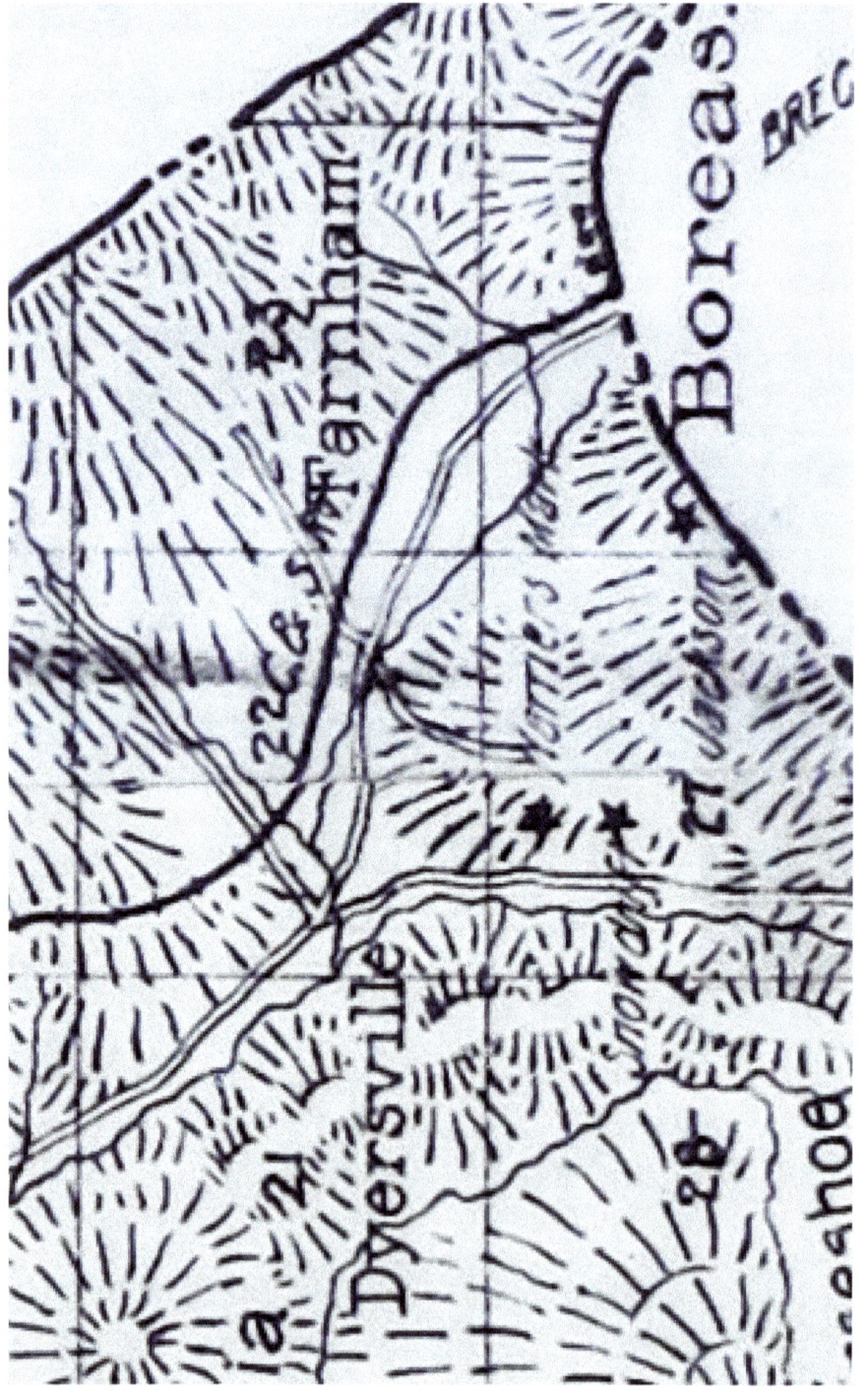

Figure 6-1. Fred Cramer Map with Dyersville, the Warrior's Mark and Snow Drift Mines, 1906. (Author's Collection)

Dyersville Townsite Location

Dyersville (sometimes spelled Dyerville), named for itinerant minister Father John Lewis Dyer, could be found in upper Indiana Gulch. In the summer of 1881, it had one saloon, a clothing store, school, and several residential cabins. No historic photographs of Dyersville have been found. Today remnants include one cabin without a roof, footprints with a few logs from three other cabins, and a roofless stable in excellent condition just outside of the town. Dyersville today meets the true definition of a ghost town.

Figure 6-2. Father John Lewis Dyer. (Courtesy of the Summit Historical Society)

Warrior's Mark Mine

The story of Dyersville actually begins with the discovery of the Warrior's (Warriors) Mark mine.

Father Dyer had become a very proficient prospector by the late 1870s. He relied on "dowsing," learned from Cornish miners years earlier when he lived in Wisconsin. Most people relate dousing to finding water. In truth, an expert in dousing can locate much more, including minerals as Dyer did.

Dyer wrote about discovering the Warrior's Mark mine in his autobiography, *Snow-Shoe Itinerant*:

> "... Being well acquainted with the mountains and mining, I was paid good wages for locating claims. When the snow was deep, I went on snow-shoes, always feeling that a preacher had a right to earn his living if he could not get it by preaching; but no right to leave his charge.
>
> My practical knowledge made my services as a locater in demand. Sometimes I gave them to deserving young fellows, whom fortune had used roughly. Two such were Candell and Thompson. In the spring of 1880 they came to me for information. Snow was more than knee deep. They were out of money, except enough to board them a few days, and put up a log pen ten or twelve feet square, just large enough for them to stand up in and make a stopping place. The next thing was a job of work. I was employed to sink holes on some claims, to hold them, and gave them employment. I bought tools for them, and we started up the mountains, I leading. Soon the trail gave out, and we broke a path in snow waist deep. We carried picks, shovels, tent, and blankets. It was hard climbing for the boys; but they said; 'If that old man can get there, we must.' And we did. I showed them where to dig. That day they had a shaft three feet deep, and slept in it at night.
>
> They worked for some time, making fair wages—say three dollars per day—and then they and myself took up some ground in company. They also continued to work and prospect for themselves

through the summer. Thompson found some float mineral, and followed it up to where it came up to the grass roots, and sunk a hole on it ten feet deep, and threw out several hundred pounds of rich mineral, gray copper, worth five hundred dollars to the ton. He staked his claim—one hundred and fifty by one thousand five hundred feet. He did know how rich it was, and let one Parkinson have a fourth interest for one hundred dollars, and would have sold the balance for two hundred and fifty dollars, but his man failed to come to time. He kept the location a secret. I had not asked him where it was, but said: 'You have got on my claim, I suspect.' He replied: 'You have no claim up there.' I answered: 'I prospected up there three years ago, and left my shovel to hold my claim.' 'Where is your claim?' he said. I inquired if he had been at the head of a certain ditch. 'Yes,' was his answer. 'Well,' I replied, 'my claim crosses about thirty rods above that.' 'My claim,' he said, 'is not within three hundred feet of that.'

I rode up, and found my shovel; and just up the hill-side I saw his corner stake, and followed to his works. I was pleased with his show for a lode, and was glad for his sake. Seeing the ground was vacant on each side of his claim, before I left I staked one claim south and four north of it. Unable to do the work myself, I took two or three pieces of his ore home with me, and told an assayer where it came from, and that I had staked the ground adjoining; and, as I had to attend to my church building, proposed to let him go in with me, if he liked the show; he to do my work for an interest. He went, and was pleased, and we made a contract. He looked at Mr. Thompson's prospect, and wanting some one to do the work, I suggested Thompson, as he would want to keep an eye on his own claim. He said nothing about buying the claim. When Thompson came in to our house, I told him they wanted to see him; and knowing that he had offered his claim for two hundred and fifty dollars, advised him, if they wanted to buy him out, not to sell for nothing. My wife named a thousand dollars, as it was easier to fall than to raise. He went and asked them twelve hundred; but they offered him a thousand, ten per cent down and the rest in sixty days. He returned in a few minutes with his hundred dollars, and said it was the first time he had ever had that much at once. Then they wanted to see Mr. Parkinson, but told Thompson not to tell how he sold. Mrs. Dyer said: 'You tell Mr. Parkinson to come here as he goes, and I will post him.' He came, and then sold his fourth for five hundred dollars, ten per cent down. There were four of the company, and so they had the big thing, and—by doing the work agreed on—three-fourths of mine also.

The ore was very rich—from low grade to a thousand dollars a ton. But one of the parties assayed some of it and showed me the certificate. It was so low that I never said a word to Mr. Thompson about it. I was disappointed in it. If anybody knew it was rich, it was those who bought it. In a day it was all over the camp that the boys had been swindled, the ore being fabulously rich. And, as a matter of course, the discoverers felt bad over the loss of a good thing. Everybody asked why they did not have it assayed. Because they had no money to pay on a risk, as but very few had received any benefit by the assays, and many considered it money out. Parties told them they were swindled, and that the sale could be set aside, and that on certain conditions they would have it done. What those conditions were I never knew. They were not to have anything except they could prove fraud, and so get the property back. So they went to law.

I had been asked by the assayer if I wished to have some of the Warrior's Mark lode assayed. I replied; 'No, I have no interest in the lode.' Afterwards he called me in and showed me his report on it, and it was lower than I had thought possible. I thought no more about it at the time, until after the sale. When they had me on the witness-stand, they questioned me as to the assay I had seen. I told them what I knew of it. 'Did you tell either of the parties before the sale?' 'No.' 'Why did you not tell them?' 'Because I was taken back, and thought it would do them no good.' This showed that they were not influenced by the assay. So the purchasers held the diggings, and the poor boys got no more. They were advised to compromise with the first party, but they would not.

Now the company went to work, but soon winter is on, and snow anywhere from five to eight feet deep. Some good mineral was raised; but the water was strong, and they concluded to sell. The price was put at three hundred thousand dollars for the whole, including my interest. I was to have eight thousand, five hundred.

About the 1st of January, 1881, I began work on a log house. Had a good horse and sled, six miles away, at Breckenridge. Selected a place to build, and taking my horse, with chain and whiffle-tree, went eight rods, mid-sides in snow, and dragged in the first tree. And so, cutting and hauling logs, and going back home each day, returning to work in the morning with lumber, I finished my house. It was seventeen feet by seventeen, a story and a half in height, shingle roof, two floors and doors. By the 19th of February I moved my wife and the last of our goods. By that time I had a hole against the bank in the snow to stable my horse. Laid poles on the snow, and put pine-brush for roof, and he was comfortable till his slab stable was built. We were within a half mile of the Warrior's Mark Lode, which was the center of attraction for mining experts and speculators. Men would come, and look, and send experts; and then others would come. All wished to make money. Some would levy blackmail, under threats of spoiling the sale. After all the efforts, the property was not sold.

The weather becoming good, they hired a superintendent and about fifty men, and resumed work. In six months they took out, as well as I could learn, between seventy-five and eighty thousand dollars. During this time, they stocked the property at three millions. After one dividend, it failed to pay any more for a time under the management. I took ten thousand dollars in stock for my part. At this time I began to look at the stock system, and concluded to let that be the last stock I would ever have anything to do with in mining. For these reasons: First, the amount is put at three times its worth; second, there are directors, clerks, and treasurer, president, superintendent, and bosses, all on pay, besides the hands. These, with mismanagement, wire-working, whisky, cards, and fancy women, beat the average lode. After several attempts to get pay out of the mine, a man took the property to work. He had secured more than half the stock, and had the control. He bought mine. I realized two thousand dollars . . ."

Of course, Dyer, here, referenced the Warrior's Mark mine.

Dyer mentions it was in the spring of 1880 that he, Candell, and Thompson located the Warrior's Mark lode. However, an article in the *Summit Daily Journal* on May 3, 1879, states: Father J. L. Dyer . . . has at last struck it rich in his mining claim near the Warrior's Mark. The entire community rejoices over his success in this venture and none more heartily than the *Journal*. He deserves it for his untiring zeal as the pioneer preacher of his church and the distinguished services he has rendered as a citizen." Other accounts place the year as 1879.

John Daugherty explains:

"The Warrior's Mark mine was discovered in 1879, about a tenth of a mile Southeast of the site of Dyersville. The discovery was a very rich vein of lead, silver and gray copper. Father J. L. Dyer had an interest in the Warrior's Mark, based on his part in the location of the mine . . .

The Warrior's Mark, throughout the winter [1880-81], attracted everyone, from mining experts to scoundrels attempting blackmail. In the spring of 1881 'they' (Dyer's word) hired a superintendent and 50 men to work the mine. In six months, according to Father Dyer, $75,000 to $80,000 had been extracted from the mine.

The 'they' Father Dyer referred to was the Warrior's Mark Mining Company, incorporated according to the laws of Colorado, in June 1881. Their capital was listed as $3,000,000, made up of 300,000 shares at $10 per share. The company officers were: G. Puterbaugh, president; J. A. Cammett, vice-president; J. M. Conway, secretary; and W. Kellogg, treasurer. All were residents of Breckenridge …"

Father Dyer's Cabin

Little appears in the old newspapers regarding the beginning of Dyersville. Not platted, the town probably started in the spring and summer of 1881with random log cabins built on both sides of Indiana Creek by the miners working at the Warrior's Mark mine. The town just sort of evolved slightly downhill from the mine but within walking distance.

Dyer began constructing his log cabin on January 1, 1881. The family occupied the cabin on February 19th. During the summer of 2006, Fountain and Rich Skovlin attempted to find Father Dyer's cabin. They searched Dyersville, climbed the wooded hillside to the Warrior's Mark mine, and explored along the stream but found nothing remotely resembling the cabin as described by Dyer. As they drove along Boreas Pass Road, Fountain suggested looking in the trees toward the stream. They split up, each carrying a hand-held radio for communication. About 20 minutes later, Fountain found remnants of a log cabin matching Dyer's description. They also found a log corral.

In the summer of 2021, Eric Twitty, owner of Mountain States Historical, and Bill Fountain explored the Dyersville site, Warrior's Mark mine, and the remains of Dyer's cabin. **Figure 6-3** comes from his report.

Twitty wrote:

"Dyer decided to erect a simple log cabin within a short distance of Dyersville and the new mine, to keep track of events. Shunning the townsite and its saloons and boom atmosphere, he chose a site in forest to the northwest, approximately one-half mile from the mine. Commuting from Breckenridge daily in the mild winter of 1881, he assembled a story-and-one-half log cabin 17'x17' in plan with two doors. Dyer also cobbled together a temporary stable for his horse, replacing it with a more permanent but still primitive structure constructed with sawmill slabs. Dyer and his wife apparently used the cabin periodically for several years, but still called

Breckenridge their permanent home. Discussed here are remnants of a cabin and stable that are almost certainly Dyer's.

Although Dyer never documented the exact location of his cabin, circumstantial evidence strongly suggests that the remnant is his. The distance from the mine is about right, the cabin size is the same, and an outline of a stable is immediately downslope. Also, Dyer harvested local trees for the cabin and cut the largest that were adjacent to the final location. Some of the stumps around the remnant are 3' to 5' high, indicating that the trees were cut while snow was still deep. In addition, a reconnaissance survey of the area around Dyersville found no other sites that match. The cabin has been reduced to a platform while the stable is marked by a footprint of log posts and footers, all of which constitute an archaeological site."

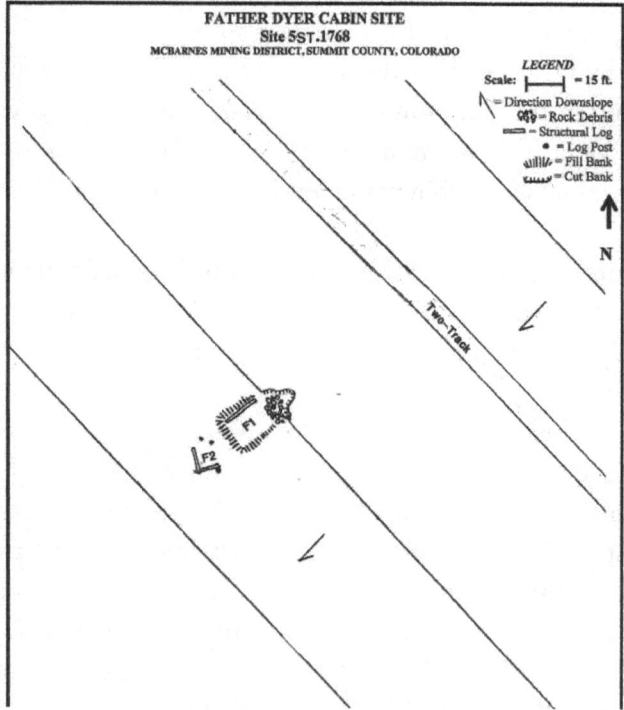

Figure 6-3. Site Map with the Remains of Father Dyer's Cabin. (Courtesy of Mountain States Historical)

Figure 6-4. Remnants of Father Dyer's Cabin, 2020. The cabin, hidden in the trees less than a quarter of a mile north of Dyersville, measured 17 feet by 17 feet. (Photograph by Author)

Figure 6-5. Father Dyer's Cabin, 2020. (Photograph by Author)

Figure 6-6. Can Dump located near Father Dyer's Cabin, 2020. (Photograph by Author)

Figure 6-7. Rich Skovlin at Corral near Father Dyer's Cabin, 2006. (Photograph by Author)

Angels Rest

In spring, 1881, Jerry Krigbaum built a saloon on the east side of Dyersville named "Angels Rest." Krigbaum, a part-time prospector, had previously lived in Conger's Camp about a mile northwest of Dyersville where he owned and operated a general store. (*Daily Journal,* June 13, 1881) The newspapers carried more news about the very popular Angels Rest than it did about Dyersville.

Krigbaum hosted lavish holiday parties at Angels Rest. The *Daily Journal* of December 23, 1881, had this to say about his first grand holiday party:

"This being the first Christmas since the settlement of 'Angels Rest,' quite a flutter is apparent in the feathery group. The old angel, Jerry, was down in town yesterday looking up supplies for the occasion. He took a two-horse sleigh load of truck out with him, the most noticeable article was the head of a ten-gallon keg filled up full of corn juice and well-surrounded with turkey, eggs, cranberries, oysters, butter, pickles, etc., etc., in too great a variety to mention. The old angel wants it generally known that they will have just the best lay-out to be found on that day and everybody will be welcome..."

In 1971, Mark Fiester visited Dyersville and the Angels Rest log building. He commented that the can and bottle dump had already been thoroughly worked by "the devotees of bottle-hunting—and what a rich treasure that dump must have provided." He added that large wooden boxes, once used for cupboards in the dilapidated structure, indicated that Wedding Breakfast Coffee was the favorite non-spirituous beverage of the establishment.

Figure 6-8. Jerry Krigbaum's Angels Rest at the Northern End of Dyersville, looking West, 1975. (Courtesy of the Summit Historical Society)

Figure 6-9. Angels Rest, looking West, 2020. (Photograph by Author)

Figure 6-10. Large Can Dump below Angels Rest, 2020. Bottle hunters over the years have thoroughly combed through the dump. (Photograph by Author)

Figure 6-11. A Salt or Pepper Shaker made from a Baking Powder Can, Angels Rest Can Dump, 2020. (Photograph by Author)

Figure 6-12. A Colmen's USA Starch Can found in the Dump, 2020. (Photograph by Author)

Figure 6-13. A Prince Albert Tobacco Can, Angels Rest Dump, 2020. (Photograph by Author)

Dyersville never enjoyed a post office. Krigbaum tried in December, 1881, but it appears the U.S. Postal Service would not open another office because Conger's Camp, about a mile to the northwest, and Farnham, a half mile to the east, both had post offices. (Conger's Camp became Argentine in January, 1881.)

The March 24, 1882, issue of the *Daily Journal* detailed one of the lavish parties at Angels Rest:

"An angelic jamboree comes off tonight at the 'Angles Rest' up among the clouds near Boreas, the occasion being the removal of the old he-angel's ten gallon keg from one log cabin to another. It is proposed by the unfeathered gang to make music in the air that will take the lead of that celestial concert of which all have read. Sorry that our reporter cannot take a balloon view of the affair as it would no doubt be worth reading."

Blue Front Clothing Store

L. Adamson, who owned the Blue Front clothing store in Breckenridge located on the northwest corner of Ridge Street and Lincoln Avenue, opened a store in Dyersville in the early 1880s. He advertised in the *Daily Journal*: "In transit from San Francisco for the Dyersville house, a choice line of California clothing and underwear. I have on exhibition at Dyersville a line of substantial well-made miners boots and gum goods that are selling on sight. Clothing at the Dyersville store at bed rock prices. Prospectors, miners and others intending to outfit are invited to call upon L. Adamson at the Blue Front, Dyersville or Breckenridge. Our motto to 'raise the standard and lower the price' will be strictly adhered to. Goods, delivered free."

The town seems to have gained a second saloon in May, 1884, with John Zwergel proprietor. (*Daily Journal*, June 7, 1884)

Dyersville Deserted

When the Warrior's Mark mine closed, residents deserted the town. The *Daily Journal* waxed poetic in reporting the sad news on July 25, 1885:

"Dyersville better known as Angel's Rest is one of the early wrecks of a late civilization, wholesale store buildings and saloons are not

> only deserted but by the accumulated snows have been crushed to earth and there remains but the crushed timbers to tell of their former existence."

Some people remained though, according to voting records. Precinct No. 11 reported that residents cast three votes in the1885, 1887, and 1889 elections.

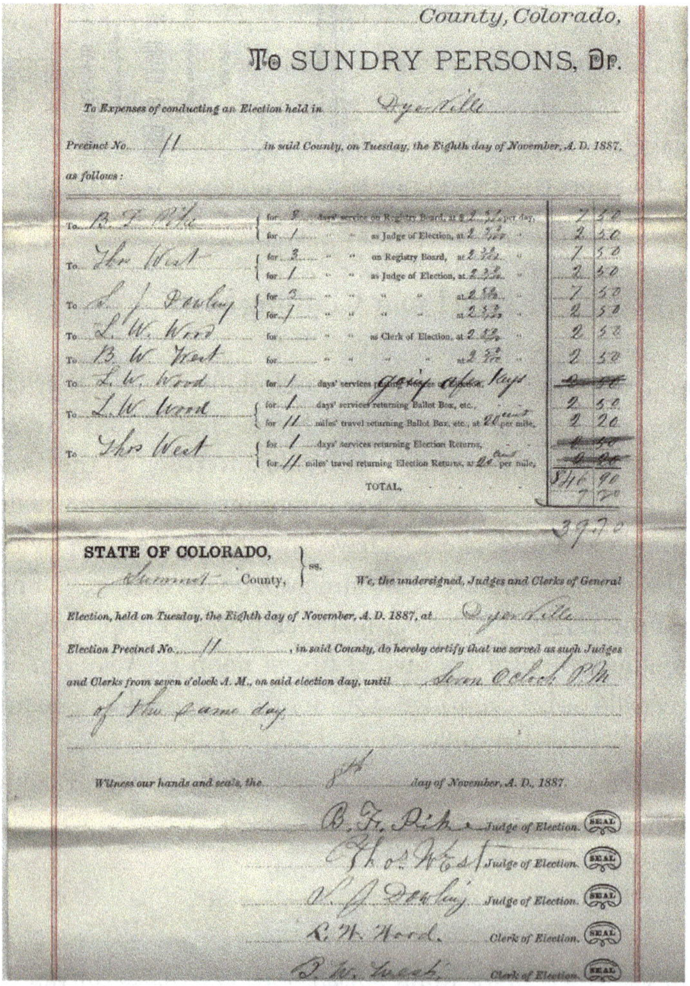

County, Colorado,

To SUNDRY PERSONS, Dr.

To Expenses of conducting an Election held in Dyersville

Precinct No. 11 in said County, on Tuesday, the Eighth day of November, A. D. 1887, as follows:

To B. F. Pike	for 3 days' service on Registry Board, at 2 50 per day,	7 50
	for 1 " " as Judge of Election, at 2 50 "	2 50
To Thos West	for 3 " " on Registry Board, at 2 50 "	7 50
	for 1 " " as Judge of Election, at 2 50 "	2 50
To S. J. Dowling	for 3 " " " " at 2 50 "	7 50
	for 1 " " " " at 2 50 "	2 50
To L. W. Wood	for " " as Clerk of Election, at 2 50 "	2 50
To B. W. West	for " " " " at 2 50 "	2 50
To L. W. Wood	for 1 days' services going after keys	~~[illegible]~~
To L. W. Wood	for 1 days' services returning Ballot Box, etc.,	2 50
	for 11 miles' travel returning Ballot Box, etc., at 20 cents per mile,	2 20
To Thos West	for 1 days' services returning Election Returns,	~~[illegible]~~
	for 11 miles' travel returning Election Returns, at 20 cents per mile,	~~[illegible]~~
	TOTAL,	$46 90
		7 20
		39 70

STATE OF COLORADO, Summit County, } ss.

We, the undersigned, Judges and Clerks of General Election, held on Tuesday, the Eighth day of November, A. D. 1887, at Dyersville Election Precinct No. 11, in said County, do hereby certify that we served as such Judges and Clerks from seven o'clock A. M., on said election day, until Seven O'clock P.M of the same day.

Witness our hands and seals, the 8th day of November, A. D., 1887.

B. F. Pike Judge of Election. (SEAL)
Thos. West Judge of Election. (SEAL)
S. J. Dowling Judge of Election. (SEAL)
L. W. Wood Clerk of Election. (SEAL)
B. W. West Clerk of Election. (SEAL)

Figure 6-14. Dyersville Judges and Clerks of Election, November 8, 1887. B.F. Pike and Thomas West served on the Registry Board and as Judges of Election; S.J. Dowling as Judge of Election; and L.W. Wood and B.W. West as Clerks of Election. (Author's Collection)

Warrior's Mark Mine

Figure 6-15, a portion of an 1882 USGS survey map with Dyersville incorrectly identified as a post office, includes lode claims above (south) of the town such as the Warrior's Mark, Snowdrift, and Mary B. The Snowdrift (Snow Drift) placer site, Mineral Survey (MS) No. 3221, partially covered the Dyersville townsite.

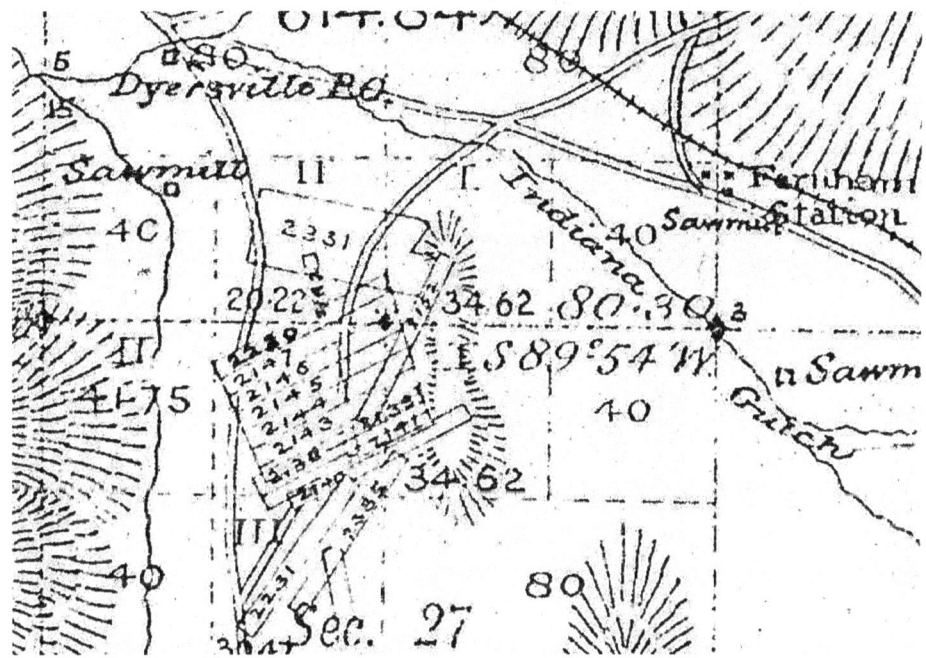

Figure 6-15. Portion of a USGS Survey Map with Claims comprising the Warrior's Mark, Snowdrift, and Mary B. Mines, July 15, 1882. (Author's Collection)

That company filed Mineral Survey (MS) No. 2138, Warrior's Mark Lode on December 20, 1881 (**Figure 6-16**); Mineral Survey (MS) No. 2139, Warriors Mark No. 2 Lode, January 6, 1882 (**Figure 6-17**); Mineral Survey (MS) No. 2140, Queer Name No. 1 Lode, January 4, 1882; Mineral Survey (MS) No. 2141, Queer Name No. 2 Lode, January 4, 1882; Mineral Survey (MS) No. 2142, Aetna Lode, January 13, 1882; Mineral Survey (MS) No. 2143, Casandra (Cassandra) No. 1 Lode, January 12, 1882; Mineral Survey (MS)

No. 2144, Casandra No. 2 Lode, January 12, 1882; Mineral Survey (MS) No. 2145, Casandra No. 3 Lode, January 12, 1882; Mineral Survey (MS) No. 2146, Casandra No. 4 Lode, January 13, 1882; and Mineral Survey (MS) No. 2147, Casandra No. 5 Lode, January 13, 1882.

In the same area George J. Washburn et al. filed Mineral Survey (MS) No. 2152, Snowdrift Lode on January 13, 1882; B.M. Newcomb et al. filed Mineral Survey (MS) No. 2230, Mary B. Lode on January 10, 1882; B.M. Newcomb et al. filed Mineral Survey (MS) No. 2231, Ridge No. 1 Lode on January 16, 1882; John Klinefelter filed Mineral Survey (MS) No. 2331, Snowdrift Placer on February 21, 1882; C.S. Barber et al. filed Mineral Survey (MS) No. 2285, Orphan Boy Lode on May 5, 1882; and Ira A. Cammett et al. filed Mineral Survey (MS) No. 2335, Bert Lode on May 6, 1882.

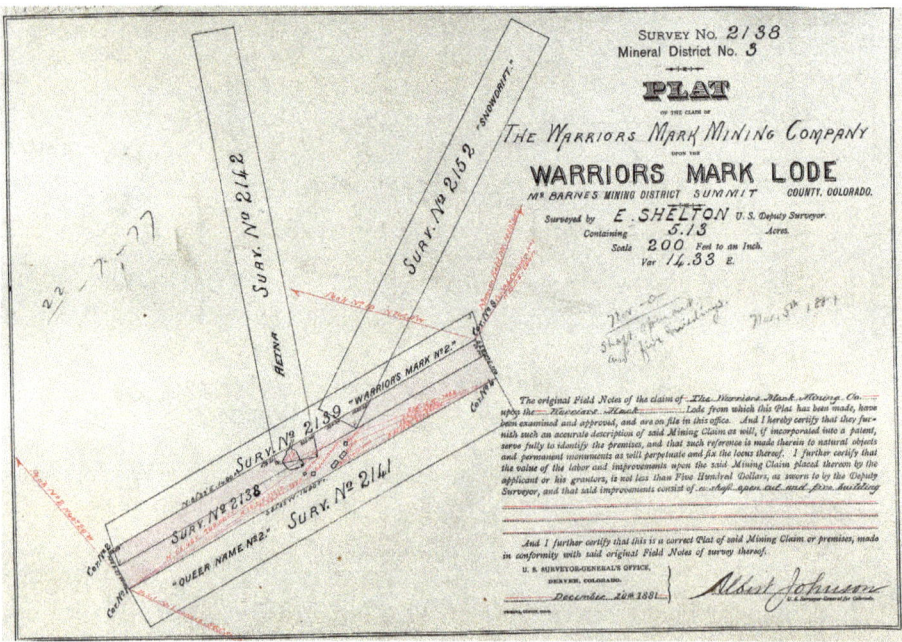

Figure 6-16. Mineral Survey (MS) No. 2138, Warriors Mark Lode, filed on December 20, 1881. Note the large open pit mine. (Courtesy Bureau of Land Management)

Chapter 6 Dyersville

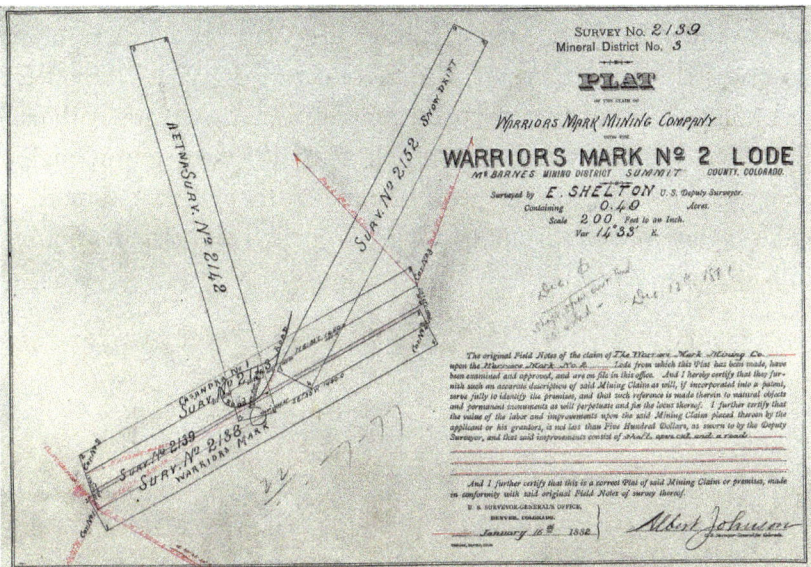

Figure 6-17. Mineral Survey (MS) No. 2139, Warriors Mark No. 2 Lode, filed on January 6, 1882. (Courtesy Bureau of Land Management)

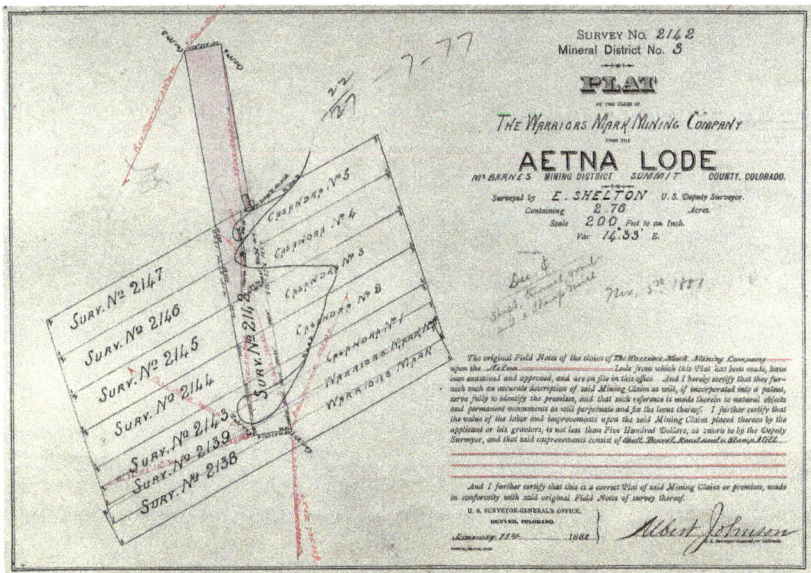

Figure 6-18. Mineral Survey (MS) No. 2142, Aetna Lode, filed on January 13, 1882. The mill can be seen in the middle of the lode, just above the Casandra (Cassandra) No. 5 lode. (Courtesy Bureau of Land Management)

By November 5, 1881, a stamp mill at the Warrior's Mark mine neared completion. The 1883 *Colorado Mining Directory* described the 60-foot by 40-foot mill as containing stop-boxes, bundles, and five stamps, with facilities to put up ten more; motive power supplied by a 35-horsepower engine and ample boiler; capacity 30 tons per 24 hours. Although owned by the same individuals, the Warrior's Mark Mining Company's property did not include the mill or equipment.

Figure 6-19. Warrior's Mark Mill Ruins, looking South, 1961. (Western History Department, Denver Public Library, X-17827)

Figure 6-20. Warrior's Mark Mill Ruins, looking West, 1961. Two concentration tables can be seen in the center of the picture. (Western History Department, Denver Public Library, X-17831)

Figure 6-21. Warrior's Mark Mill Ruins, looking South, 2019. Little remains after 60 years. Note the two concentration tables seen in Figure 6-19. (Photograph by Author)

Figure 6-22. Warrior's Mark Mill Ruins, looking North, 2009. (Photograph by Author)

Daugherty added: "The Warrior's Mark was patented in 1881 or 1882. The mine was developed by an open cut 35 feet long and 35 feet deep and 25 feet wide. It also had two shafts, one 55 feet, the other 67 feet. The ore from the Warrior's Mark was processed in the Aetna concentrator [mill], which was not a part of the Warrior's Mark Company, but under the same ownership.

The company should have been doing very well, as the amount of silver per ton ran from 1,030 ounces per ton to 6,000 ounces per ton. The ore average $100 per ton or $4,000 per rail car load."

Burchard in an 1881 USGS report concluded that the Warrior's Mark mine produced nearly $40,000 in ore from the open pit. He continued: "The Snow Drift is in the same vicinity and is taking out considerable rich ore, which is piled on the dump, no shipments having yet been made."

Snowdrift and Mary B. Mines

Daugherty provided details:
"The Snowdrift [often spelled Snow Drift] Mine was located in March 1881 and patented in February 1882. The claim was located on Indiana Creek adjoining the Warrior's Mark. The original strike consisted of two fissure veins with pay streaks, one varying from 15 to 20 inches, and the other from one to four inches. Twenty-five to 150 ounces of silver were taken per ton of ore. The owners were G.J. Washburn of Denver, and A.S. Hall and J.L. Klinefelter of Breckenridge.

Developments included five shafts from 60 to 150 feet deep and two tunnels, 75 and 100 feet long. An engine house with a 17-horsepower engine, a hoist, and other buildings constituted the Snowdrift's mine.

The Snowdrift Placer, adjoining the Snowdrift Mine, was located in 1881 and was in the process of being patented in 1882. The owners [of the] Snowdrift Mine also owned the placer. Developments included 300 feet of flume and a quarter mile ditch.

The mine was taking out ore in 1881 but was storing it in a dump. Possibly the owners were waiting for the completion of the Denver, South Park Line to make ore shipments easier. In 1883, a 165-foot shaft was sunk and plans were made to install a pump (a #5 Knowles) to keep the shaft drained. Through 1885, the Snowdrift evidently prospered, as regular shipments of ore were made, and late in 1885 it was planned to install a stamp mill. After 1885 I lost track of the Snowdrift, but it evidently played out . . ."

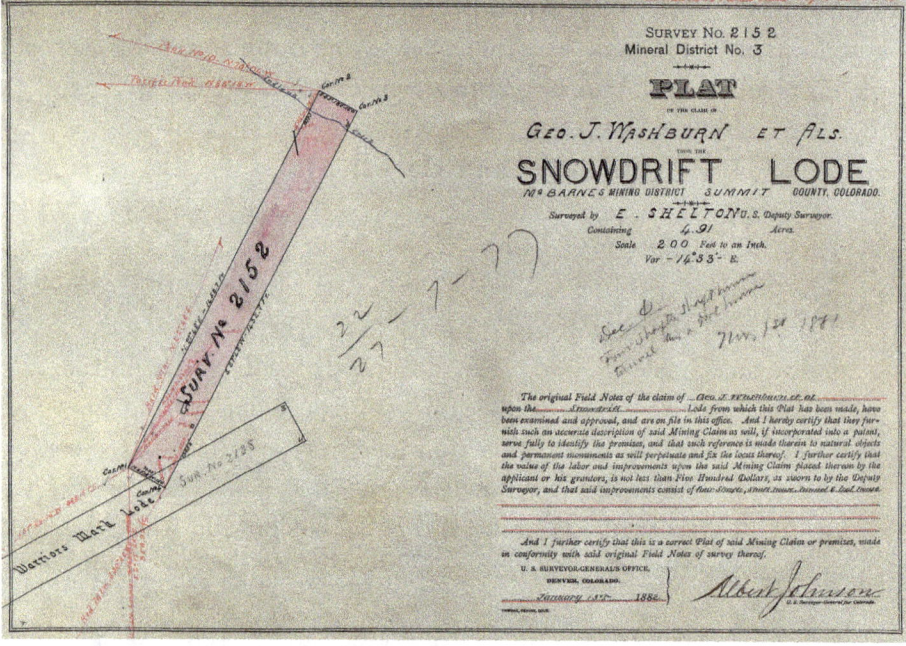

Figure 6-23. Mineral Survey (MS) No. 2152, Snowdrift Lode. (Courtesy Bureau of Land Management)

Chapter 6 Dyersville

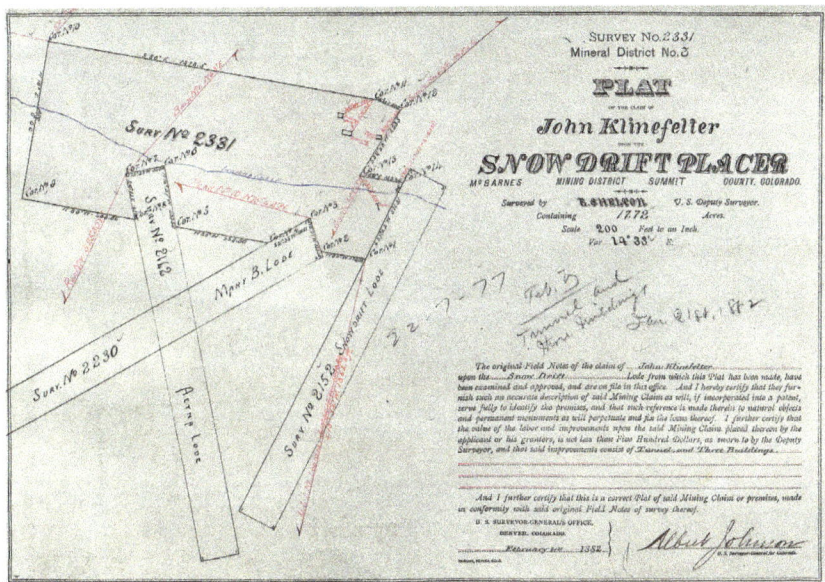

Figure 6-24. Mineral Survey (MS) No. 2331, Snowdrift Placer, filed on February 21, 1882, by John Klinefelter. The three buildings (Dwelling House, Boarding House, and Bunk House) in the northeast corner of the claim, just north of Indiana Creek and written in red, would have been in the Dyersville town limits. (Courtesy Bureau of Land Management)

Figure 6-25. Snowdrift Shaft Dumps, 2009. (Photograph by Author)

Figure 6-26. Collapsed Snowdrift Shaft, 2009. (Photograph by Author)

Figure 6-27. Wire Cable near the Snowdrift Shaft, 2009. (Photograph by Author)

Miners at the Mary B. mine (**Figure 6-28**), located adjacent to the Warrior's Mark, used the Mary B.'s 14-foot shaft to uncover a 7-foot vein of minerals. (*Fairplay Flume*, January 12, 1882) Assays ranged from $12.80 to $2,876 per ton for the extremely rich vein of gray copper. The Warrior's Mark mill processed the ore. (**Figures 6-19, 6-20, 6-21, 6-22**)

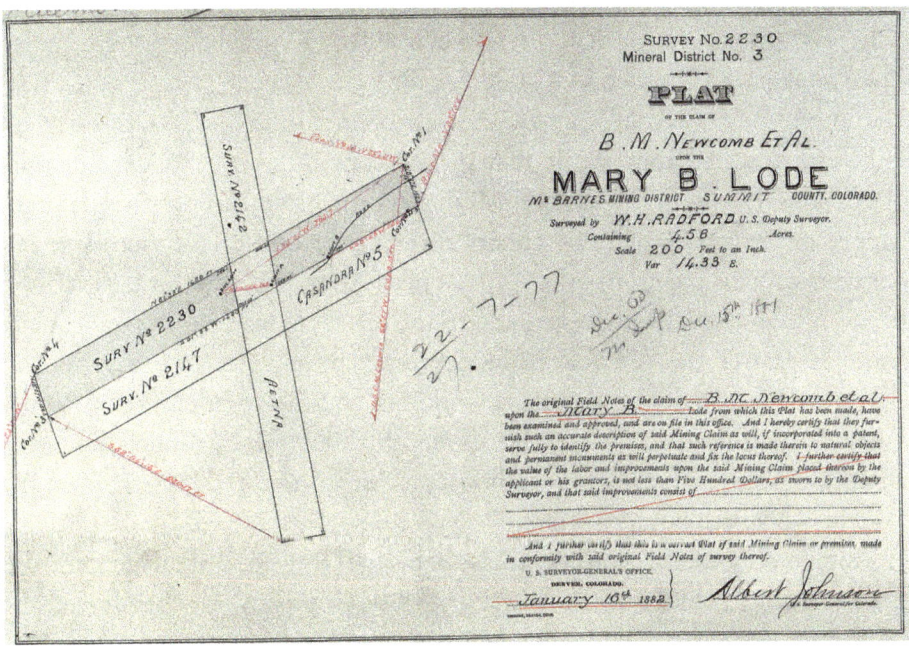

Figure 6-28. Mineral Survey (MS) No. 2230, Mary B. Lode. (Courtesy Bureau of Land Management)

Warrior's Mark Mine

Daugherty continued: "By 1882, a sawmill had been constructed [at the Warrior's Mark mine] for the purpose of further development of the mine. One hundred thousand dollars worth of precious metals had been extracted."

In September, 1883, Cecil C. Morgan, with a reputation as one of the best mining men in the state, took charge, installed new equipment, "fired up" the mill, and removed as much as 70 feet of water. After the miners struck a well-defined vein, they shipped four carloads of first-class ore. By the middle of October, Morgan employed over 30 men with Mr. Boylan as foremen.

Two months later, the miners intercepted a pay streak about three feet wide, assaying about $300 per ton. The company anticipated employing two shifts of six throughout the winter to mine and sort the ore but would wait until spring to concentrate and ship it to Denver using the Farnham station of the Denver, South Park, located about a half mile away.

By December, the work force numbered 16; the gray copper and native silver ore assayed as much as $2,000 per ton.

The 1883 *Colorado Mining Directory* explained that the Warrior's Mark mine's veins were "from two to fifty inches, containing gray copper in a porphyry gangue, the first-class ore milling, when sorted, twenty-five per cent copper and from 500 to 1,000 ounces silver, the second-class from five to ten per cent copper and from 50 to 250 ounces silver, and the third-class from five to fifty ounces silver per ton, and in the other claims a similar ore gangue and vein-matter; the Warrior's Mark developed by an open cut thirty-five and sixty-seven feet in depth, and other workings, and the other claims by twenty other shafts from ten to fifteen feet in depth, 2,000 feet of tunnels, and other workings; improvements—ore-houses, shaft-houses, etc.; output from the Warrior's Mark about $96,000."

Problems loomed according to Daugherty: "But good management did not solve the problem of the Warrior's Mark Company, for they leased the mine to James Fryer and Colonel Morgan, who obtained a bond on the controlling interests. James Fryer [from Baltimore] then purchased the Bank of Breckenridge . . . He sent for his son in Baltimore to run the Bank. In June 1884, Fryer purchased the Warrior's Mark for $100,000. But Mr. Fryer was evidently not the most honest or thrifty individual that ever lived. In 1885, the Warrior's Mark was in the hole financially to the tune of $19,000. Eight thousand dollars was owed to the Warrior's Mark employees. James Fryer evidently tried to slip out of Breckenridge with money taken from the Warrior's Mark woman cook, but was caught. Fryer was forced to restore the cook's funds, but what happened to him is unknown . . . In May 1885, John M. Denison filed suit in the U. S. Circuit Court against the Warrior's Mark Mining Company for $41,000. A few days later, the petition of C. H. Bacon, Warrior's Mark stockholder, to plead and contest the judgment until Bacon and other petitioners could plead their case. Another suit was won by the German National Bank of Denver by default. The judgment in this suit was for $1,225. I found no further information on either case as to the reasons for the suits and their final outcome. However, I would not doubt it if Mr. Fryer had a hand in the reasons for the suits."

Daugherty continued: "The Warrior's Mark Mine operated fairly steadily until 1900. From 1889 through 1896, the Warrior's Mark Stamp Mill (15 stamps) constructed in 1884, was listed under Farnham in the Directories."

The *Mining News* reported on September 8, 1900, that a crew of 14, working under Charles Lipplet, produced rich ore and completed some development work.

Financial problems arose: From 1904 through 1906, the Warrior's Mark group of mining claims, including the Warrior's Mark lode, Warrior's Mark No. 1 lode, Cassandra lodes Nos. 1-5, and Queer Name lodes Nos. 1 and 2. appeared on the Summit County delinquent tax list.

The *Summit County Journal* followed changes at the Warrior's Mark: new equipment, a new manager—Mr. Morgan, an inspection revealing "a pay streak of about three feet in width that ran about $300 to the ton. The advice given was to keep at least two shifts of six men at work all winter and carefully sort the ore and ship the best at once to Denver, and when the season opens next year concentrate the balance. In that way the old miner aforementioned thought the Mark would again come to the front as a valuable and steady producer."

The *Breckenridge Bulletin* printed this legal notice on November 4, 1908:

"Treasurer's Notice Complying with a Request for Notification so as to Become Entitled to a Tax Deed. Law of 1905 . . .

Aetna Lode . . . Cassandra No. 1 Lode . . . Cassandra No. 2 Lode . . . Cassandra No. 3 Lode . . . Cassandra No. 4 Lode . . . Cassandra No. 5 Lode . . . Queer Name No. 1 Lode . . . Queer Name No. 2 Lode . . . Warriors Mark No. 1 Lode . . . Warriors Mark No. 2 Lode . . ."

Other legal notices followed (*Breckenridge Bulletin*, February 20, 1909): "Treasurer's Deed—George Robinson to Maurice Hilderman: Cassandra Nos. 1, 2, 3, 4 and 5; Queer Name Nos. 1 and 2; Warriors Mark Nos. 1 and 2 in McBarnes district."

"Treasurer's Deed—George Robinson to Maurice Hilderman: 1/8 Snow Drift lode and 1/8 Snow Drift placer and improvements in McBarnes district."

"Treasurer's Deed—George Robinson to Maurice Hilderman: Three-fourths Snow Drift, three-fourths Snow Drift Placer and improvements in McBarnes district."

The Warrior's Mark mine faded from the newspaper for several years. But interest in the mine didn't die. On April 19, 1909, J.B. Look, superintendent of the Illinois Central Mining and Milling Company, wrote George Robinson, Summit County treasurer at the time, asking the status of the claims. Had they been sold for taxes? Would it be possible for him to learn the address of the present owner of the claims? A second letter from Look to the treasurer on May 1, 1909, stressed the urgency of the request.

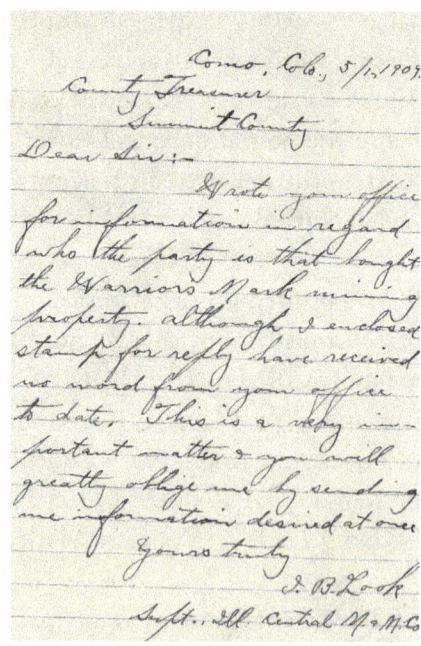

Figure 6-29. Letter from J.B. Look to Summit County Treasurer's Office concerning the Warrior's Mark Mining Property, May 1, 1909. (Author's Collection)

Chapter 6 Dyersville

Again, the mine disappeared from the *Journal*, reappearing September 20, 1919, with exciting news. The Warrior's Mark Mining Company had been incorporated by Samuel Klous of Boston, Massachusetts, along with Robinson, and William Keogh, Summit County assessor, both living in Breckenridge. With a capitalization of $1 million and shares selling for $1 per share, the company had hired men to clear tunnels for development work. The property consisted of the Warriors Mark; Warrior's Mark No. 2; Queer Name; Queer Name No. 2; Aetna; Cassandra Nos. 1, 2, 3, 4, 5; Mary B.; Snowdrift and Snowdrift placer.

On February 21, 1920, the stockholders met in Denver and decided to increase the capital stock of the company from $1 million to $5 million. A work force had been working since the previous summer clearing debris from the tunnels. Miners found an ore streak assaying over $500 per ton in silver and about 40 percent lead. They expected to reach the main contact using a cross-cut tunnel. (*Summit County Journal*, May 15, 1920)

The optimism reached Leadville's *Herald Democrat*, when, on December 6, 1921, it reported that a streak of ore about eight to ten inches in thickness and valued at about $10,000 per ton had been found on the 100-foot level of the mine.

Not wanting to be left out, the *Summit County Journal* on December 31, 1921, reviewed the recent history of the Warrior's Mark:

> "In November the new drift, started east from the old 625-foot deep Warrior's Mark shaft at the 'hundred-foot level,' encountered a vein of high-grade silver ore which will probably sell for about $300 a ton if fairly closely sorted. The pay ore streak varies from ten to fourteen inches in width and has proven to be fairly regular as it is followed to the east. By picking out the high-grade nodules or chunks of bright silver ore some very high assays (from 1,700 to 4,000 ounces of silver per ton) can be obtained. The second, or 150-foot level, has been put in good condition for working, another drift has been opened and cut the silver vein at that level. At 60 feet from the shaft the pay-streak is said to be eighteen inches wide. New work is also planned, probably at greater depth, from the lower portions of the incline shaft, which is an incline from the 150-foot level to the bottom. It is expected that a carload of the ore will be shipped early in the New Year."

The newspaper announced new operators for the Warrior's Mark and 7-30 mines in September, 1923: the Aco Mining and Leasing Company of New York. George Robinson directed the operations at the Warrior's Mark with C.M. Glasgow the engineer in charge. Samuel Klous of Boston financed the company.

Unfortunately, Klous died unexpectedly on September 3, 1923, at the Denver Hotel in Breckenridge of acute intussusception of the bowel. His death stopped further development of the Warrior's Mark. (According to Google, intussusception of the bowel occurs when a part of the intestine slides into an adjacent part of the intestine. This telescoping action blocks food or fluid from passing through.)

By the end of 1923, water had totally flooded the Warrior's Mark, up to the collar; the mill sat in ruins.

Columbine Vein/Shaft

Twitty made a remarkable discovery at Warrior's Mark Mine in 2021.

"Today, the Warrior's Mark Mine is an archaeological site featuring the early 1880s open-cuts, the circa 1883 Warrior's Mark Shaft, and remnants of workers' housing. The Warrior's Mark Tunnel is downslope and north, recorded along with the mill ruins and Columbine Shaft as 5ST.377. As a site, the Warrior's Mark Mine is in mixed condition. The open-cuts, which were the main point of production, are distinct and obvious, but somewhat slumped in. The Warrior's Mark Shaft was capped during 2003, and the activity avoided the adjacent building platforms and foundations representing the surface plant. The large crew that developed the open-cuts and shaft lived in a group of cabins and boardinghouses southeast of the workings, and although the buildings and structures are gone, a well-preserved set of platforms marks each one.

The Warrior's Mark Mine has been recorded for this project as site 5ST.1767, a Smithsonian number that SHPO provided to clear up conflicts with earlier work. In particular, both the real Warrior's Mark Mine discussed here, and the Columbine Shaft around 500' to the north, were registered as site 5ST.377, even though they were completely separate sites. In 1974, local interests mistook the Columbine Shaft for the Warrior's Mark Mine, and registered it as 5ST.377. The information on the site form was very sparse, as was common for the era, and photographs depicted what is actually the Columbine Shaft. With the wrong name and no clear location information on the form, SHPO assumed that 5ST.377 was the Warrior's Mark site as labeled on topographic maps.

In 2003, DRMS visited the real Warrior's Mark for a closure project, and applied the number 5ST.377. DRMS documented almost no content regarding the site and recommended it not eligible. Uncertain about the site's significance, SHPO officially determined it as Need Data. Around 2003, DRMS closed the Warrior's Mark Shaft with a polyurethane foam plug inset within the collar, preserving the site's integrity as it was. The result was no adverse effect. After an explanation of the above conflicts in 2021, SHPO assigned 5ST.377 to the Columbine Shaft based on its geographic association. To differentiate the Columbine Shaft from the real Warrior's Mark Mine, SHPO then assigned 5ST.1767 to the latter."

Therefore, for the last 50 years the Columbine vein and shaft house have been misidentified as the Warrior's Mark shaft and shaft house. (**Figures 6-47, 6-48, 6-49**) The USGS map in **Figure 6-32** identifies the Columbine vein.
Twitty described the Columbine Shaft:

"The Columbine Shaft site features three closely spaced components from the greater Warrior's Mark Mine operation. Investors bought the Warrior's Mark claim group in 1880, organized the Warrior's Mark Mining Company in 1881, and produced silver ore from several large open-cuts (5ST.1767). Within the year, they expanded the operation and sited two important additions on the Aetna claim, around 500' north of the open-cuts. One was the Warrior's Mark Tunnel, which the company planned to drive around 600' southeast and reach the vein beneath the open-cuts, for development at depth. The other was the Warrior's Mark

Mill, relying on a battery of stamps and mercury amalgamation to recover silver and gold from the ore. The tunnel was never finished and the mill was largely a failure, even after being refitted around 1883 and in 1885. Also, the company began sinking the Columbine Shaft on a vein by the same name, but this too was left incomplete until the mid-1880s, when a little ore was mined. In 1919, the Warrior's Mark Mines Company finally drove the tunnel to its destination and encountered enough ore to support regular output for a few years. Shortly afterward, the company also improved the Columbine Shaft and generated more ore, contributing to an overall successful operation. The mill on the other hand saw no further use after around 1885 . . .

The Columbine Shaft, Warrior's Mark Tunnel, and Warrior's Mark Mill were components of the greater mine by the same name. The description of the Warrior's Mark Mine (Site 5ST.1767) includes a full history that includes the tunnel and mill, but archival sources make little mention of the Columbine Shaft. Mineral claim survey plats depict a small prospect shaft at the location, which the Warrior's Mark Mining Company sank on the Columbine Vein. Either the company began developing it around 1883 or successor James H. Freyer did so in 1884, and produced a little ore. One of the two parties also erected a shaft house enclosing a hoisting system. But it was the Warrior's Mark Mines Company that conducted the most work, rehabilitating the shaft house and hoisting system around 1921, and developing the vein to a greater extent."

Twitty continued his description: (Refer to **Figure 6-30**):
"F1 - Originally, the shaft (F1) was vertical, supported by closed-type hewn log cribbing, and 4'x8' in-the-clear. The collar was framed with a timber set almost flush with the surrounding ground. After abandonment, the shaft imploded around 50' below the surface, causing a subsidence funnel that pulled down the cribbing as a structure. The funnel is approximately 20' in diameter that drew in surrounding ground, with the shaft structure still at the center.

Chapter 6 Dyersville

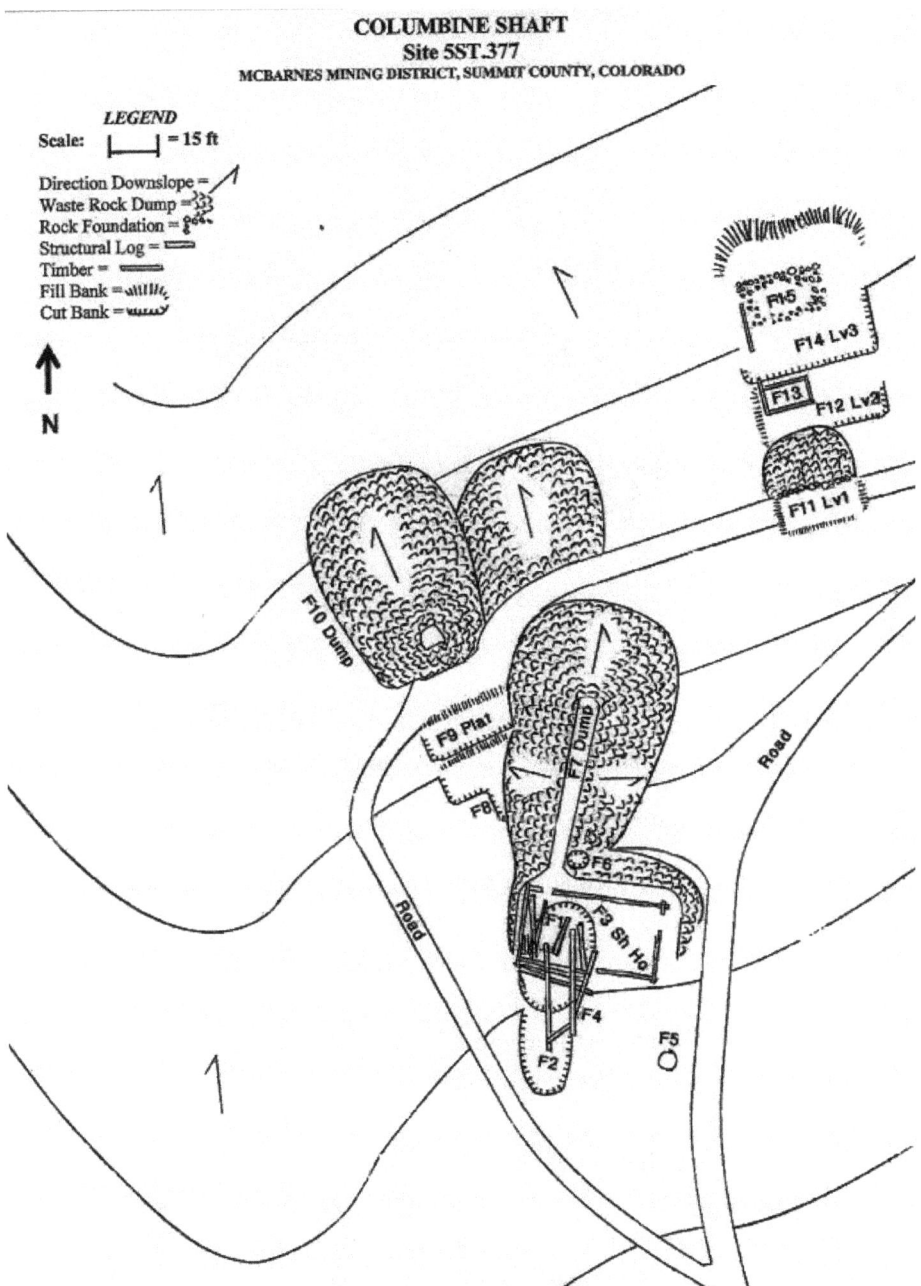

Figure 6-30. Columbine Shaft Map. Note the Warrior's Mark tunnel (F8), shaft (F1), and mill (F11-F15). (Courtesy Mountain States Historical)

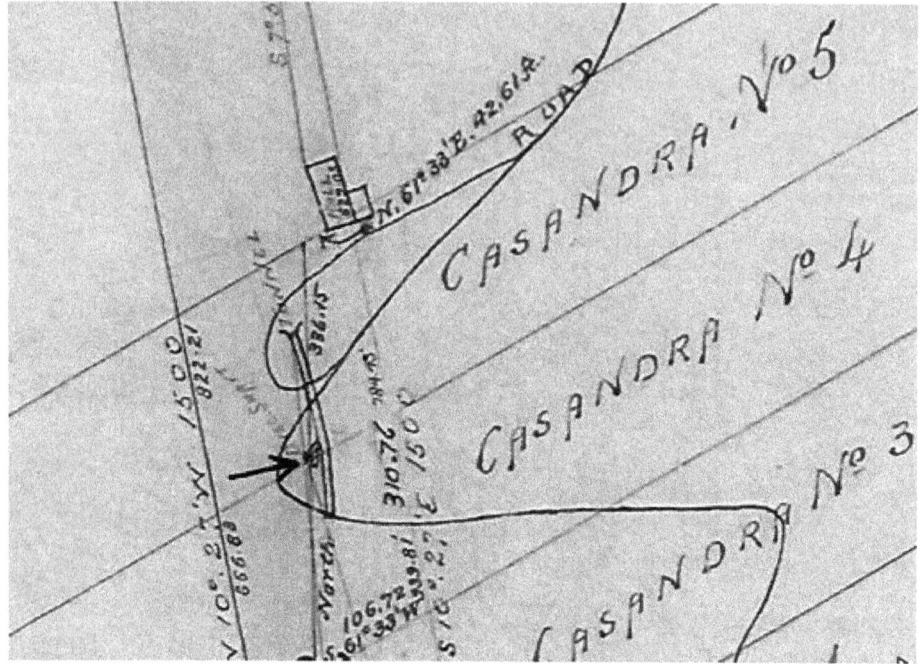

Figure 6-31. A Portion of the Warrior's Mark 1881 Mineral Claim Survey Plat. The arrow points to the Columbine shaft (Figure 30, F1). (Courtesy Mountain States Historical)

F2 - The vein extended south from the shaft, and miners extracted the ore from top to bottom. They hollowed out a linear stope (F2) that was around 4' wide, vertical, and opened just beneath the surface. The walls later imploded and created a linear area of subsidence 15' wide, 30' long, and 25' deep. The subsidence features fresh scarring from recent settling.

F3 - A stout log shaft house (F3) enclosed the shaft collar, a hoisting system, and a blacksmith shop. Now a ruin, the building was a rectangular block 26'x39' in plan on a pad of waste rock. Workers used already downed, full-length logs for their stability, and assembled them with well-made square-notch joints. Chinks were sealed with mud and split wood strips. It remains unknown what the building's roofline was, but it was lofty and had a cupola to accommodate the headframe's high crown. The shaft was in the southwestern quarter, which was undermined when the collar slumped in. The hoist was in the northeastern quarter as confirmed by grease-stained boards, but absence of a proper foundation suggests that the machine was a free-standing donkey unit. The blacksmith shop was in the northeastern quarter, and a thick deposit of anthracite coal and forge clinker remains. The building's northwestern corner had a broad doorway so that miners could shuttle waste rock out in ore cars, while the northeastern corner had another doorway for the shop. The building collapsed decades ago, the walls falling outward and the roof dropping into the interior. The western wall still stands intact, and is 8' high. The shaft house features a characteristic artifact assemblage that includes structural materials, blacksmithing refuse, general hardware, and cable lengths. Wire nails were used to assemble all primary woodwork, while cut nails are scattered around. A few hole-in-cap cans with lapped side-seams, sanitary cans, and carbide drums are scattered downslope. The cut nails and hole-in-cap cans reflect initial development during the early 1880s.

F4 - The headframe (F4) stood over the shaft, and was a two-post gallows type 8'x13½' in plan and 25' high, with backbraces descending east toward the hoist. The structure has since toppled south as a mostly intact unit. For the upright posts and backbraces, workers hewed full-length logs into 10"x14" timbers, and were so skilled that the timbers almost appear to have been milled. The structure stood on a foundation of 12"x12" hewn timber footers straddling the shaft. The timbers were assembled with mortise-and-tenon joints, and the crown, with braces for the sheave wheel (gone), was reinforced with iron tie rods. When the headframe was standing, its crown peeked above the shaft house roof, and was enclosed in a cupola. Remnants of the cupola, clad with corrugated sheet iron, are still attached to the headframe.

F5 - A prospect pit (F5) exists upslope from and southeast of the shaft house, and was probably adapted as a privy vault. The pit is 6' in diameter, 2' deep, and filled with earth.

F6 - A second prospect pit (F6), also likely used as a privy vault, is north of the shaft house. The pit is 5'x6' in area, 3' deep, and covered with earth and duff.

F7 - When miners sank the shaft, they dumped waste rock (F7) east across the mountainside, spreading out a pad of fine material 30'x55' in area. The pad then became a platform for the shaft house. As they developed the underground workings, they used ore cars to dump additional waste rock to the north, building up a lobe 76' long. Ultimately, the entire formation became 50'x106' in area and 9' thick."

He described the Warrior's Mark tunnel:

"The Warrior's Mark Mining Company began driving the tunnel southeast to intersect the vein underneath the mine's main open-cuts, 600' away. The company erected a basic surface plant limited to a tunnel house enclosing the portal, a blacksmith shop, a timber dressing station, and an ore bin. A rail line exited the tunnel and passed through the building on its way out to the waste rock dump. As noted, the company never completed the tunnel, but the Warrior's Mark Mines Company finally bored it to the Warrior's Mark Shaft, and the vein, in 1920.

F8 - At one time, the tunnel portal (F8) was around 4'x6' in-the-clear and penetrated loose ground, which miners reinforced with log timbering. The woodwork later rotted and the portal imploded, becoming a subsidence trench 7' wide and 15' long, now partially buried with waste rock from the shaft above.

F9 - A tunnel house (F9) enclosed the tunnel portal, and it was 30'x35' in plan and featured three levels. A blacksmith shop was located on the upper level, which was 10'x15' in area. The middle level, 10'x30' in area, had a timber dressing station and an sorting station, where workers manually removed waste. They threw the material into a parked ore car, and dropped recovered payrock into a holding bin below, which was the bottom level, similar in size.

Wagons traveled a one-way loop road and stopped at the structure's base and took on sorted payrock for shipment. The building was completely dismantled more than a century ago, leaving the three stairstep platforms, which are blanketed with earth, duff, and waste rock, promoting the growth of spruce trees. Cut nails, remnants of plank flooring, and other debris remain.

F10 - As workers processed payrock in the tunnel house, they shoveled separated waste (F10) into an ore car parked within the structure. When it became full, they pushed the car out and northwest along a dead-end trestle and emptied it. Over time, they built up two mounds, the eastern being 38'x42' in area and the western 45'x62' in area and 6' thick."

USGS Report

A 1951 USGS report entitled *Geology and Ore Deposits of the Upper Blue River Area Summit County, Colorado, Geological Survey Bulletin 970*, completed in 1940-1942 by Quentin D. Singewald, contained information about the Columbine vein:

"The Columbine vein has every surface indication of strength and values comparable to the Warrior's Mark but without the enriched network of stringers which resulted in the open cut on the latter vein."

The report added:

"The Warrior's Mark mine is located at the head of Indiana Gulch between the east and west forks of Indiana Creek, 7 miles southeast of Breckenridge. A wagon road, passable for trucks in 1941, connects the mine with the Alma-Breckenridge highway. The mining property includes 14 claims, which are peppered with prospect pits, shafts, and adits. No underground workings were accessible in 1940 and 1941, but information gleaned through surface study by the writer has been supplemented by data from a private report prepared by Berger and Sayre (1923) and by information furnished by George Robinson, of Breckenridge, Col . . .

Subsequent to surface mining in the open cut, the Warrior's Mark shaft was sunk 90 feet vertically and then 470 feet inclined along a vein dipping steeply to the northwest. Berger and Sayre state that the 65-foot level is supposed to extend 50 feet to the southwest and 35 feet to the northeast but was caved in both directions . . . On the northeast side a sample of soft material 6 inches wide ran 343.8 ounces silver and a paying amount of copper . . . A grab sample of . . . ore caved into the level [southwest of the shaft] . . . ran 14.90 ounces silver and pay copper. Above the cave a streak at the back 4 inches wide ran 453.50 ounces silver. This was the extent of underground sampling possible in the Warrior's Mark."

Berger and Sayre added that the Shaffer tunnel "is connected with the old Snow Drift workings, which show but little ore." According to Robinson, the 165-foot level from the Warrior's Mark shaft "supplied much ore, some of it from under the open cut . . ."

Chapter 6 Dyersville

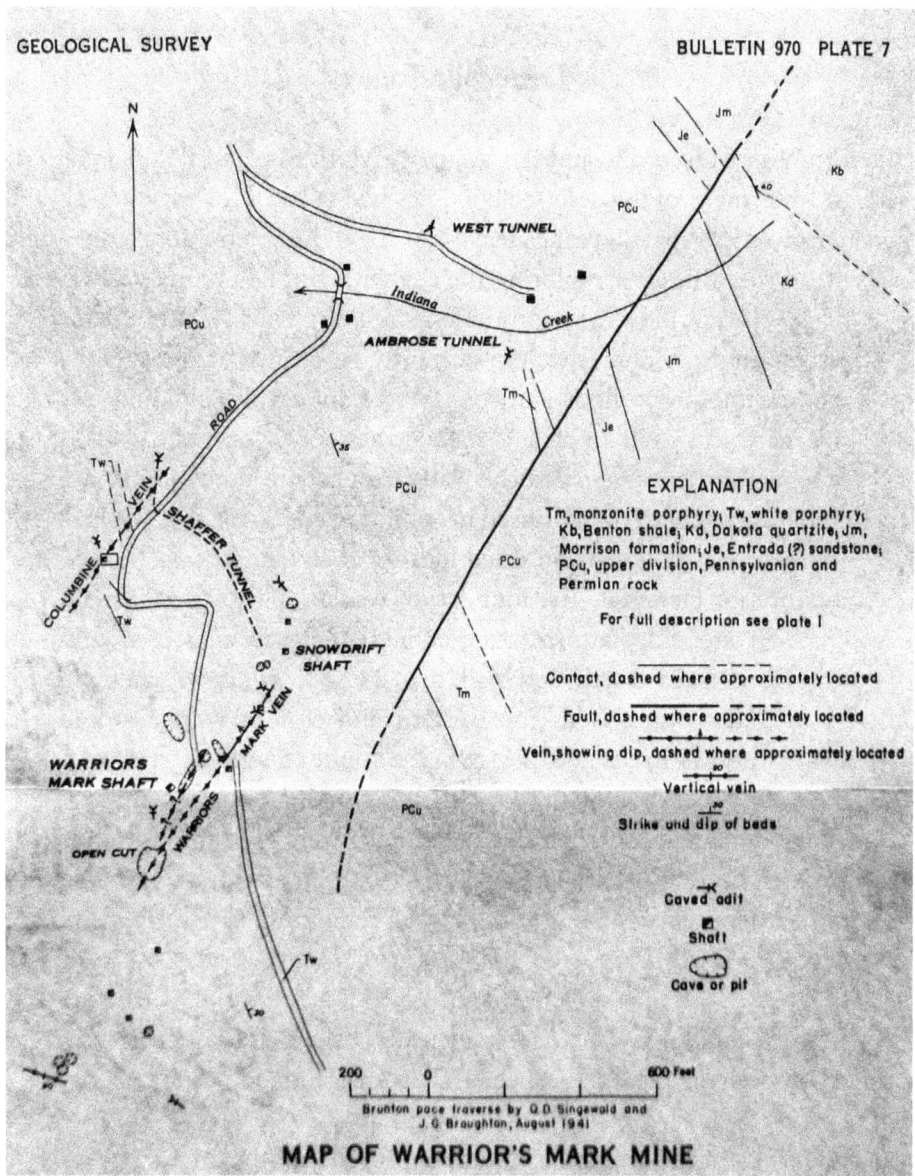

Figure 6-32. USGS Map of Warrior's Mark Mine and Surrounding Area, 1941. The map includes the Warriors Mark vein and shaft; Snowdrift shaft; Columbine vein and shaft; Shaffer tunnel between the Columbine vein and Snowdrift shaft; and Ambrose tunnel near the Dyersville townsite. (*Geology and Ore Deposits of the Upper Blue River Area, Summit County, Colorado, Geological Survey Bulletin 970*)

Dyersville Today

The fortunes of Dyersville and the Warrior's Mark rose and fell together. As early as 1885, many of the deserted buildings had fallen. However, some buildings remained in 1961, 80 years later. Since then, the deterioration continues.

Twitty wrote this after exploring the site with Bill Fountain:

"F1 - Dyersville's most prominent building ruin (F1) housed a restaurant or saloon. The ruin currently features four intact walls that are missing a floor and roof. When intact, the building was side-gabled, 18'x29' in plan, 8' high at the roof eaves, and consisted of logs. Workers assembled the walls with square-notch joints and chinked gaps with mud pressed in behind plank forms. The workers chose already downed and dried logs for their stability, and hewed the interior faces flat. The foundation was no more than logs laid on a cut-and-fill platform large enough the building's footprint. The front faced north and had two 24"x65" windows and two 33"x72" doorways. Both the western and eastern walls featured twin windows in 50"x60" frames. The foundation is deteriorated, the walls suffer dry-rot and are missing chinking, and the windows, doors, floor, and roof are gone. Wire nails were used for all woodwork, reflecting rehabilitation after 1890. Artifacts are few and buried deposits are absent. A collapsed cellar pit 8'x10' in area and 4' deep is north.

F2 - The building's (F1) toilet was a privy upslope and east. Currently, the underlying pit (F2) is open, 4'x7' in area, and 4½' deep.

F3 - A third commercial building stood on the main street's western side. The building was mostly dismantled decades ago, and the remaining debris was then widely scattered around. A platform (F3) 30'x40' in area currently outlines the building, and although the platform is overgrown with ground-cover, foundation elements are visible along the western side. The elements include a full-length log footer and two collapsed rock stacks. No artifacts are visible.

Chapter 6 Dyersville

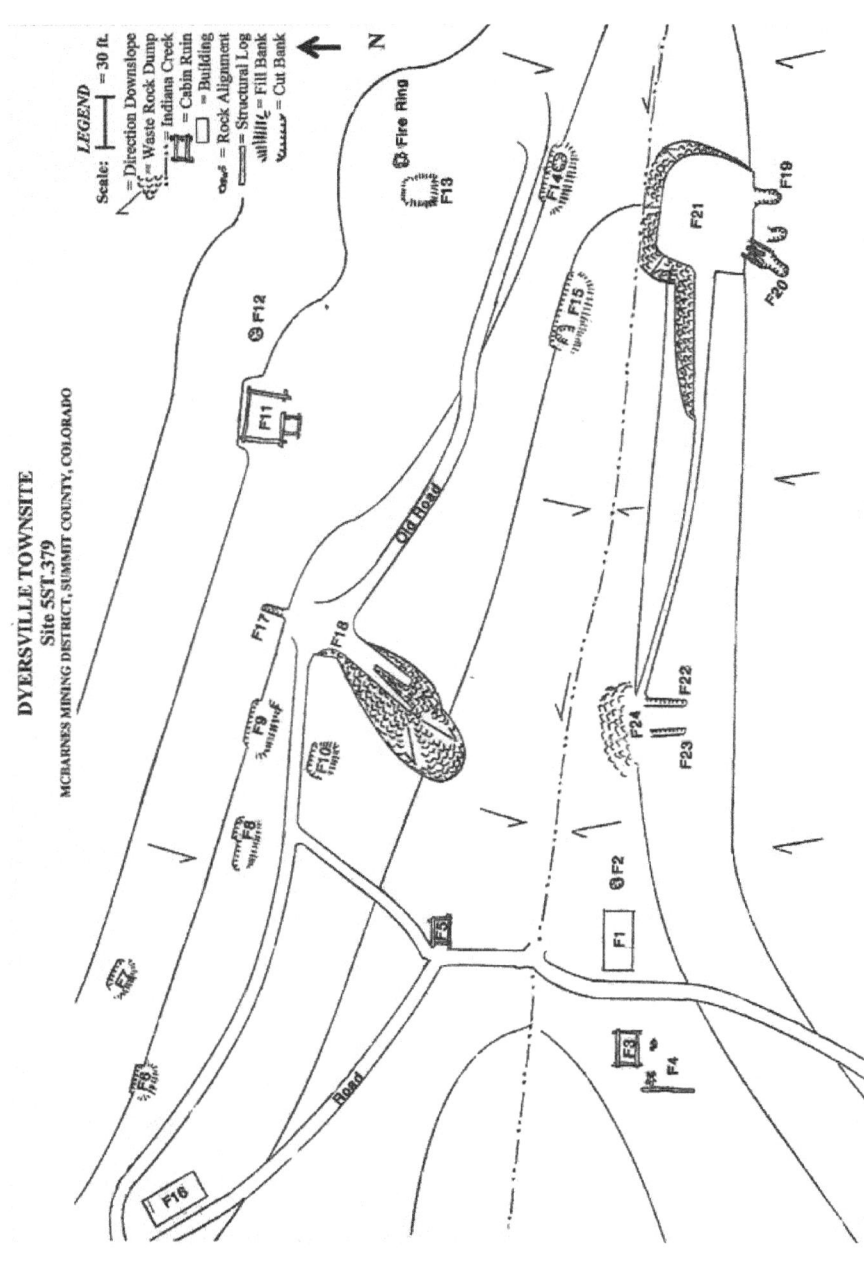

Figure 6-33. Site Map of Dyersville. (Courtesy of Mountain States Historical)

The residential district confirmed to a loose grid anchored to a road contouring the gulch's northern wall. Currently, platforms and foundations account for nine lodging businesses and residential cabins, although more were certainly present during the town's peak.

F5 - A small residential cabin stood on the creek's northern side, north of the business district. When complete, the cabin was front-gabled, 12'x15' in plan, and consisted of logs assembled with V-notch joints. The foundation (F5) was an outline of logs on a platform just large enough for the cabin's footprint. Wire nails were used for all woodwork. The walls are now gone, leaving an outline of logs around structural debris, which is most of the artifact assemblage.

F6 - The western-most cabin was just above and north of a main road passing through the townsite. The building is gone, and now outlined by a cut-and-fill platform (F6) 15'x18' in area. The platform is well-formed, surrounded by spruce trees, and features a handful of general domestic artifacts.

F7 - The second western cabin was much like the first. Its platform (F7) is 15'x18' in area and poorly graded, the surface sloping south. Given this, the cabin had to be supported by additional log footers, which are missing. The cut-bank has slumped and the fill-bank is subtle, being overgrown with grass. A few cut nails are sprinkled around, and bottle and tableware fragments are mixed in with soil downslope. Shallow yard deposits are likely.

F8 - The third residential cabin stood above a road intersection, with one branch descending south to the business district and the other contouring east to more cabins. This residence was L-shaped on a cut-and-fill platform (F8) 15' wide and 30' long, with a northern extension 8'x8' in area. The location, size, and footprint suggest that cabin was a lodging business. The platform is currently subtle with faint cut and fill banks overwhelmed by ground-cover, partially concealing a shallow root cellar. A few cut nails, can shreds, and bottle and tableware fragments are widely scattered downslope. Shallow yard deposits are likely.

F9 - Near the townsite's center was a residential cabin on a prominent platform (F9) built up with earth to drain snowmelt. The platform is 18'x20' in area with a flat surface and bold cut and fill banks. The area is blanketed by ground-cover that hides artifacts, except for a handful of cut and wire nails, and bottle and tableware fragments.

F10 - One of the middle cabins was a small residence on a cut-and-fill platform (F10) 12'x15' in area. The platform is poorly formed with an uneven surface blanketed by ground-cover, which hides artifacts.

F11 - Angel's Rest (F11) was a combination restaurant and saloon erected in Dyersville's early years, and used as a residence during the late 1890s. Now a ruin, the business was a log building 22'x32' in plan on a foundation of log footers, laid over a slightly larger cut-and-fill platform. Workers assembled the logs with V-notch joints and chinked gaps with mud and log strips. During construction, workers erected a three-stall stable along the south side, integrating its logs into the cabin's walls. Gaps in the walls mark two doorways. Cut nails were used for the cabin's primary woodwork, and wire nails were added during later repairs. The cabin has completely collapsed, toppling south and dropping the roof and its loft over the interior. A domestic refuse dump extends downslope and south into a thick spruce stand, which buried most materials with duff. Regardless, numerous cans, bottle and tableware fragments, and a few general household items are visible. Hole-in-cap cans with lapped side-seams, crude bottle glass, and several bottle bases with FHGW and L. Co. marks date to the late 1870s and early 1880s. Hole-in-cap cans with inner-rolled and soldered seams, and 2-quart rectangular cans are circa 1900, while sanitary and vent-hole cans reflect the 1910s. Many cans are institutional sizes, typical of restaurants. Buried yard deposits are likely, while the refuse dump offers additional materials.

F12 - The last occupants of Angel's Rest relied on a privy to the east as their toilet. Today's privy pit (F12) is a dished depression 4' in diameter and 1' deep. The pit probably offers few buried deposits because the residents were unwilling to prematurely fill it with solid refuse, and thus dig another pit in a short span of time.

F13 - One of the townsite's eastern residences was a cabin erected on a low knoll. Experienced with mountain winters, the residents built up an earthen pad (F13) 15'x18' in area, surrounded by shallow ditches, all of which deflected snowmelt and kept the cabin dry. The platform is faint and overgrown with spruce saplings, and features the broken trunk of an old-growth tree along the eastern side. In recent years, recreationists have used the knoll as a camp, arranging a large fire pit and a bench. Artifacts are very few.

F14 - The second eastern cabin was erected early and occupied during the late 1890s. Currently, a cut-and-fill platform (F14) 18'x40' in area outlines the location, at the end of the townsite's east-west road. The platform is well-formed, features a slumped cellar pit 6'x9' in area, and had distinct cut and fill banks. The building's size and cellar pit suggest that it housed a lodging business. Decayed log footers lie around the perimeter, while structural material is jumbled near the center. Several heavy timbers with abandoned mortise-and-tenon joints are amid the debris, and were salvaged from an industrial building elsewhere. Only a handful of general domestic artifacts lies downslope. Cut nails reflect early construction, while wire nails are from later repairs.

F15 - The townsite's southeastern building might have been another lodging business. The building is long gone, but a faint cut-and-fill platform (F15) approximates its footprint. The platform is 20'x50' in area and poorly graded, with a hummocky surface sloping south toward the nearby stream. The sloped surface required additional log footers to level the building. A slumped cellar pit 7'x10' in area is in the platform's western end. Thick grass conceals artifacts, and shallow yard deposits are possible.

F16 - The townsite's stable (F16) was somewhat isolated in the northwestern corner, at the intersection of roads extending east into the residential district and southeast to the business district. The stable was also away from residences and businesses to minimize noxious odors and flies. Now a ruin with four standing walls, the stable was 14'x33' in plan on a platform cut from a steep slope. The walls are currently 8' high and consist of logs assembled with well-made square-notch joints, while gaps were chinked with log strips. The inside faces of the logs were hewn flat, and 2"x4" planks supported plank crowns 11' high. As was typical for crude frontier stables, the walls had no windows and only one low doorway, which was 33"x48" in size. The foundation was a perimeter of heavy logs, with several timber bolts reinforcing the western wall. All woodwork was fastened with wire nails. A few shreds of tack straps and hardware are scattered around. In 2010, USFS recorded the stable alone as a residential cabin and assigned it the independent number of 5ST.1340. USFS missed the fact that the building was actually a stable associated with the rest of the nearby townsite, including the two cabin platforms only a short distance to the east. The stable has been recorded again here as a feature of Dyersville.

Like other towns that began as prospectors' camps, and evolved with speculation and claim development, Dyersville includes the remnants of several exploratory ventures that undoubtedly began in the early 1880s atmosphere of optimism. But as work underground failed to find ore worth mining, the ventures went bust after several years.

F17 - One of these is the West Tunnel (F17), driven northerly to evaluate a mineralized vein on the gulch's northern wall. Prospectors found the vein by digging pits and trenches approximately 200' upslope and farther north (not recorded). At one time the tunnel was more than 200' long and timbered for support, but is now a collapsed subsidence line 8' wide and 18' long.

F18 - When driving the tunnel, miners used ore cars to dump waste rock (F18) downslope. Over time, they deposited a pair of lobes 42' wide, 130' long, and 8' thick.

F19 - During Dyersville's boom years, mining outfits drove the Snowdrift and Ambrose tunnels into the gulch's southern floor to intersect different veins underground. The Snowdrift Tunnel (F19) extended south roughly 200' and headed for the Snowdrift Vein, but encountered little of note. At one time timbered for support, the tunnel imploded and now takes form as a subsidence trench 8' wide and 18' long.

F20 - The Ambrose Tunnel (F20) angled southwest for the Warrior's Mark Vein and apparently passed into an impoverished ore-bearing zone. The low-grade material was not profitable as of the early 1880s, but attracted renewed interest during the 1900s or 1910s. At that time, the operators supported the portal with cap-and-post timber sets assembled with logs. The woodwork rotted and imploded, and the tunnel is currently a subsidence trench 7' wide, 33' long, and 6' deep.

F21 - When boring the two tunnels, miners used ore cars on a track to dump waste rock (F21) on the gulch floor. In so doing, they deposited a pad of material 60'x90' in area and 4' thick, which is overwhelmed with vegetation. The miners also used waste rock to grade a wagon road extending west.

F22, 23, & 24 - Early in the property's history, prospectors dug a trench (F23) and drove an adjacent exploratory adit (F22) south into the gulch floor, possibly as a failed start for the Ambrose Tunnel. The portal collapsed and is a trench 5' wide and 30' long.

When working the adit, the prospectors used wheelbarrows to dump waste rock (F24) at the portal, depositing a hummocky pad 36'x65' in area and 6' thick, now thickly overgrown.

The townsite has a disappointingly sparse and overly generic artifact assemblage. The business district offers almost nothing, although some items are probably just beneath the surface, concealed by sod and duff. Most of the residential platforms feature thin scatterings of cut and wire nails, bottle and tableware fragments, disintegrated cans, and a few household items. Angel's Rest has the best assemblage, with cans, broken bottles, and domestic items lying amid duff downslope and south, amid old-growth spruce trees. Dateable artifacts reflect occupation during the early 1880s, the early 1900s, and 1910s. Hole-in-cap cans with lapped side-seams, crude bottle glass, and several bottle bases with FHGW and L. Co. marks date to the late 1870s and early 1880s. Hole-in-cap cans with inner-rolled and soldered seams, and 2-quart rectangular cans are circa 1900, while sanitary and vent-hole cans reflect the 1910s. Many cans are institutional sizes, typical of restaurants."

Figure 6-34. Two Log Buildings at Southern End of Dyersville, 1961. (Figure 6-33, F3 & F1) Note the window in the large building. A mine dump appears on the right, in the background. (Western History Department, Denver Public Library, X-17834)

Figure 6-35. Similar View as in Figure 6-34, July, 1971. (Figure 6-33, F3 & F1) Again, note the window in the large building. Part of the roof remains on the building to the right. The building across Indiana Creek still stands. (Courtesy Don Winslow)

Figure 6-36. Similar View as in Figure 6-34 and 6-35, 2019. (Figure 6-33, F3 & F1) Note that the window in the large building has become a door. Little remains of the building on the right or the one on the other side of Indiana Creek. (Photograph by Author)

Chapter 6 Dyersville

Figure 6-37. Dyersville looking South across Indiana Creek, 1961. (Figure 6-33, F5, F1, & F3) (Western History Department, Denver Public Library, X-17820)

Figure 6-38. Dyersville, Similar View as in Figure 6-37, 1975. (Figure 6-33, F5, F1 & F3) (Courtesy of the Summit Historical Society)

Figure 6-39. Similar View as in Figures 6-37 and 6-38, 2009. (Figure 6-33, F5, F1 & F3) Very little remains of the cabins. (Photograph by Author)

Figure 6-40. Looking South with Indiana Creek flowing between Two Cabins, 1961. (Figure 6-33, F5 & F1) (Western History Department, Denver Public Library, X-17826)

Chapter 6 Dyersville

Figure 6-41. Cabins at the Southern End of Dyersville, 1961. (Figure 6-33, F1 & F3) (Western History Department, Denver Public Library, X-17821)

Figure 6-42. Board Cabin in the Northeastern End of Dyersville, 1961. (Figure 6-33, F14) (Western History Department, Denver Public Library, X-17829)

Figure 6-43. Footprint of Cabin in Figure 6-42, 2020. (Figure 6-33, F140) (Photograph by Author)

Figure 6-44. Ambrose Tunnel in the Northeastern Section of Dyersville, 2020. (Figure 6-33, F20) See USGS map in Figure 6-32 for location south of Indiana Creek. (Photograph by Author)

Chapter 6 Dyersville

Figure 6-45. Large Log Stable, 2020. (Figure 6-33, F16) Located less than a mile west of Dyersville "town limits" on the north side of the main road, it originally stood one and one-half stories high. The half story provided storage for hay. (Photograph by Author)

Columbine Vein and Shaft House, Shaffer Tunnel, Snowdrift Shaft

Figure 6-46. Columbine Shaft House, July, 1971. (Figure 6-30, F1 & F3) (Courtesy Don Winslow)

Figure 6-47. Columbine Shaft House, 1970s. (Figure 6-30, F1 & F3) (Western History Department, Denver Public Library, X-62431)

Figure 6-48. Columbine Shaft House, 2009. (Figure 6-30, F1 & F3) (Photograph by Author)

Figure 6-49. Collapsed Shaffer Tunnel Adit, 2020. Note location on the USGS map in Figure 6-32. (Photograph by Author)

Warrior's Mark Mine

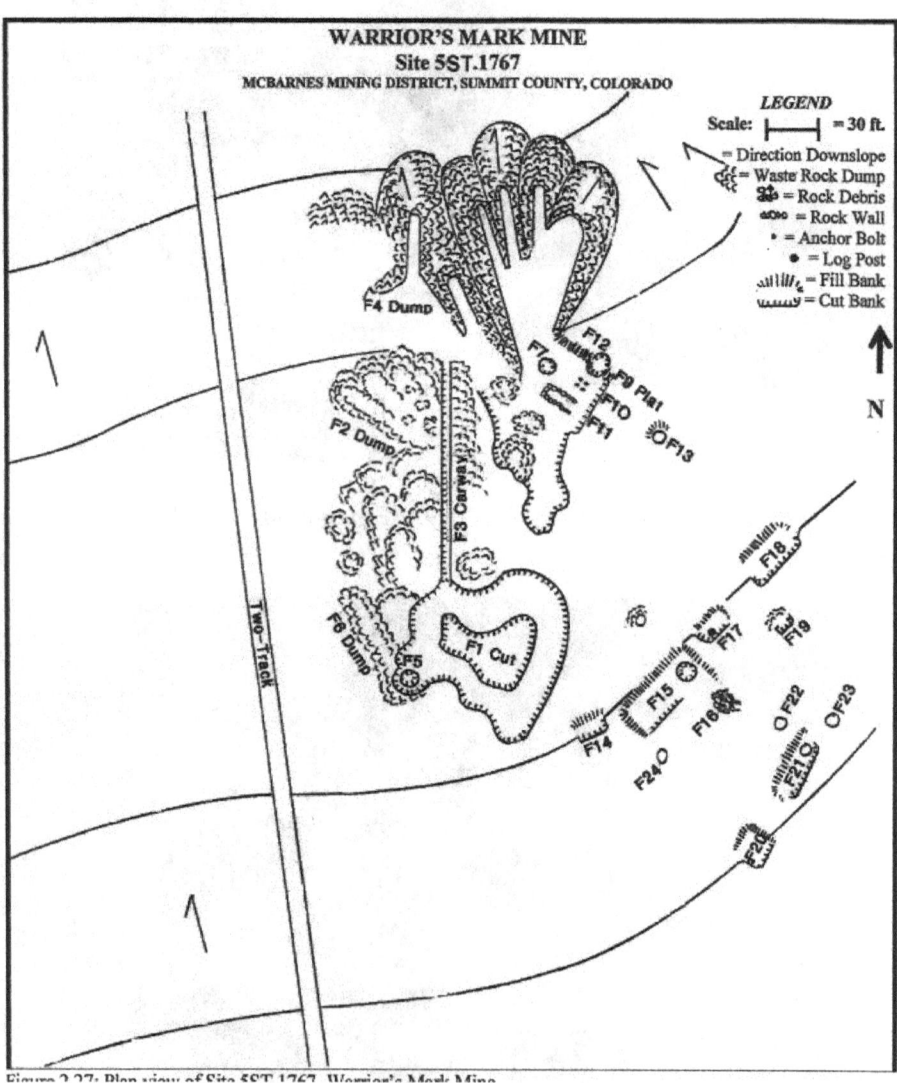

Figure 6-50. Site Map of Warrior's Mark Mine. (Courtesy of Mountain States Historical)

Twitty described the site:
   "Open Cut Workings

F1 - When the mining outfit pinpointed the vein's rich surface outcrop, they hired a crew to extract it with open-cut methods. Workers simply stripped away overburden and blasted out ore as encountered, creating an irregular chamber (F1) in the mountainside. The chamber became around 50'x60' in area featuring nearly vertical walls. With continued ore extraction, the workers deepened the chamber to around 30', whose sides gradually tapered inward. The walls have since slumped in, enlarging the rim to 90'x90' in area with rounded shoulders. Around 5' of eroded sediment now buries the floor.

F2 - As workers enlarged the open-cut, they used wheelbarrows and ore cars to dump overburden (F2) northwest. Dead-end gangplanks served as runways for the wheelbarrows, while flimsy trestles supported rail lines for the cars. Within a short time, the workers spread out a confusion of hummocky waste rock lobes and isolated mounds, one overlapping the other, covering a 70'x150' area. The mounds and lobes range from 5' to 9' in thickness, and have a rough, haphazard appearance.

F3 - As workers went deeper in the open-cut, heaving waste rock up and over the rim became impossible. To solve the problem, the workers blasted out a carway (F3) 135' to the north, so they could shuttle out waste rock and payrock in ore cars. The carway was a slot trench 7' wide with a track on a level floor. The trench walls have since crumbled in, but the trench is still clearly evident for what it was.

F4 - Once the carway was complete, workers used it to shuttle waste rock (F4) out of the cut and dump the material to the north. Over time, they deposited several lobes 75'x120' in area and 7' thick. Each lobe represents a dead-end rail spur for dumping the waste.

F5 - Miners sank a prospect shaft (F5) into the open-cut's southwestern corner, hoping to find a continuation of the ore body. The shaft was a bust and was abandoned with no formal development. When intact, the shaft was probably around 4'x8' in-the-clear and 100' deep, cribbed to support loose walls. The woodwork rotted and imploded, and the shaft became a subsidence pit 20' in diameter and 12' deep, with no original form. The shaft is thus a non-contributing element of the site.

F6 - When miners sank the shaft, they used an ore to dump waste rock (F6) to the northwest. In so doing, they created a lobe of cobbles 24' wide, 60' long, and around 5' thick. A cable pulley for an aerial tramway lies to the west. Given that the mine never had a tramway, the apparatus was probably adapted as hoist for the shaft, and left in its current location when the shaft was abandoned.

Warrior's Mark Shaft

In 1883, the Warrior's Mark Mining Company sank the Warrior's Mark Shaft to develop the vein's deeper reaches. The shaft was ultimately 600' deep but failed to encounter ore in meaningful volumes, and so was abandoned for some time. In 1919, the Warrior's Mark Mines Company drove the Warrior's Mark Tunnel to the shaft, drained it at the 200' level, and then pumped out the rest of the water. Driving drifts along the vein from the shaft, the company finally found enough rich ore to sustain several years of production. The first company installed a standard hoisting system for work at depth, including a headframe over the shaft, a powerful steam hoist, and two return-tube boilers. The system, a blacksmith shop, and timber dressing station were all enclosed in a large frame shaft house.

F7 - At one time, the shaft (F7) was vertical, 4'x8' in-the-clear, and penetrated loose ground. Miners installed cribbing to support the walls, but the woodwork rotted and imploded, creating an ant-trap funnel. During the 1990s, DRMS plugged the funnel with a plug and pushed in a small amount of ground as a cap, with a faint scar around 10' in diameter. A closure monument is at center.

F8 - As miners developed the underground workings, they used ore cars on dead-end rail spurs to dump waste rock (F8). Over time, they built up a fan of four distinct lobes 100'x130' in area and 10' thick. They kept the top-surface flat, and each lobe represents a dead-end spur. The dump is as created.

F9 - A frame shaft house enclosed the shaft, its hoisting system, and a blacksmith shop. The building is gone, but a distinct cut-and-fill platform (F9) outlines the footprint. The building was 36'x60' in plan and oriented northwest-southeast. The shaft was in the northwestern end, the hoist in the southeastern, and its boiler stood along the southwestern wall. A water tank was countersunk into the northeastern side. The platform features a typical artifact assemblage including lumber, cut and wire nails, window glass, blacksmithing refuse, and general hardware.

F10 - A square set of anchor bolts (F10) is left from the hoist. The set features a perimeter of eight bolts for the bedplate, and four more at the rear for the steam cylinders. According to the outline, the hoist was a single-drum steam unit 9'x9' in plan.

F11 - The boiler was a return-tube model in a masonry setting (F11) 8'x18' in plan. When the boiler shell was salvaged, portions of the setting were knocked over, leaving two partially standing walls, which were made with local rocks. According to the setting's size, the boiler shell was 4' in diameter and 16' long, and the firebox faced southeast. Fuel coal is scattered around.

F12 - The boiler required water, and so the company countersunk a water tank in the platform's northeastern edge. The tank was around 6' in diameter and 6' deep, and has since decayed and imploded, creating a pit (F12) 7' in diameter. Water had to be freighted to the mine because there were no nearby streams, and thus the company countersank the tank so that condensation from the hoist could be piped in for reuse.

F13 - A prospect pit (F13) lies upslope from and southeast of the shaft house platform. The pit is 6' in diameter and 4' deep, and was probably adapted for use as a privy vault. The pit is filled with earth.

Workers' Housing

In 1880 or 1881, the original Warrior's Mark company arranged a large workers' housing complex east of the open-cut. The original handful of workers built a cabin, and the mining outfit added a row of two large boardinghouses and a blacksmith shop, all at the base of a slope where meadow transitions into thick spruce forest. The outfit erected another cabin and boardinghouse upslope, for a total of six buildings. Currently, well-formed and distinct platforms outline the building footprints, the buildings themselves having been dismantled or burned.

F14 - The western-most building was a small cabin approximately 12'x15' in plan, possibly a foreman's residence. The building is long gone, currently marked by a cut-and-fill platform (F14) slightly larger in area. The surface is blanketed with sod, cut nails are sprinkled around, and bottle glass extends northwest.

F15 - The complex's second building was a large boardinghouse on a raised pad of earthen fill (F15). The building was dismantled long ago, but when intact, was 18'x50' in plan, side-gabled, and probably story-and-one-half in height. The kitchen was in an extension 15'x20' in plan. Today's platform is well-formed with a collapsed cellar pit, 10' in diameter and 6' deep, in the northeastern end. Prior to collapse, the cellar was used to store a high volume of food. The platform offers a good artifact assemblage including structural debris, fragmented liquor and beer bottles, tableware shards, food cans, and a few general domestic items. Nearly all nails are cut types and most cans are hole-in-cap vessels assembled with lapped side-seams.

F16 - A stone masonry furnace (F16) stood in the boardinghouse's eastern extension. It remains unknown if the furnace was an oven for cooking, or for assaying. The structure collapsed and is now a mound of rubble and bricks 10' in diameter and 3' high.

F17 - Blacksmithing was an essential service in the mine's first years, sharpening drill-steels and picks, and fabricating light hardware. The first-generation blacksmith shop was a simple frame building 15'x15' in plan constructed next to the boardinghouse. An anvil block on a cut-and-fill platform (F17) currently remains, and the platform is poorly formed with an uneven surface. The block was made from a spruce stump 18" in diameter with cut nails and a strap in the top to anchor the anvil. Thick sod covers the surface, but some shop refuse is visible.

F18 - The second boardinghouse was a rectangular building 18'x30' in plan, and probably story-and-one-half in height. The existing platform (F18) is a cut-and-fill pad with a light scatter of structural debris, and domestic refuse dispersed around. The refuse includes fragmented liquor and beer bottles, hole-in-cap cans assembled with lapped side-seams, and general household items. Buried yard deposits are likely.

F19 - The second boardinghouse had several privies over its lifetime, and each stood over a shallow pit that was backfilled when full. The last pit (F19) was never capped before being abandoned, and was upslope and south. The pit is well-formed, 3'x6' in area, and around 3' deep. When residents left the boardinghouse to use the privy, they carried out refuse and dumped it, leaving a concentration of food cans and general household items. Most of the cans are hole-in-cap types with lapped side-seams, and some are 1-gallon in size. Buried deposits are unlikely because the pit was shallow.

F20 - According to mineral claim survey plats, the southern building was the mine's assay office, on a platform (F20) different from the housing complex's others. The building was a cabin around 15'x15' in plan and apparently of log construction. The platform is a raised earthen pad around 16'x18' in area with ditches dug around the upslope edges. The ditches diverted snowmelt, while the elevated platform kept the cabin's foundation and floor dry. At center is a cellar pit 3'x6' in area. The platform is totally blanketed with duff, which conceals most artifacts. A high number of bricks are scattered downslope.

F21 - The eastern-most boardinghouse was north of and aligned with the assay shop. Its platform (F21) is well-formed, graded with cut-and-fill methods, and 20'x36' in area. A slumped root cellar 7' in diameter and 3' deep is in the northeastern end. According to cut nails and hole-in-cap cans assembled with lapped side-seams, the building was initially occupied during the 1880s. But miners lived in it again around 1905 and left an unusually diverse artifact assemblage featuring a variety of food cans. Types include hole-in-cap cans with inner-rolled and soldered seams, early sanitary cans with inner-rolled and soldered seams, sanitary ends with lapped side-seams, sanitary cans with vent-hole plugs, early vent-hole milk cans, key-wind coffee, ovoid sardine, and one-piece vent-hole. In general, the diverse set of containers reflects a change in canning technology, which spanned an era from around 1905-1915.

F22 - Like the main boardinghouse, the upper, eastern one had several privies as toilets. The pits were shallow and filled quickly, so the residents moved the privy building to new pits as needed. Several pits are still evident. One pit (F22) is downslope from the platform, and is 3' in diameter and filled with duff.

F23 - The second pit (F23) to the east, is 4' in diameter and filled.

The site's artifact assemblage has been reduced by natural deterioration and collection by recreationists, but still is a good representative example. As noted above, the open-cut offers few items because most activity was limited to extracting ore, and buildings and structures were few. In contrast, the Warrior's Mark Shaft complex includes structural materials and typical industrial debris, such as blacksmithing refuse, general hardware, and boiler fittings. The workers' housing complex has a diverse assemblage of early 1880s bottle fragments, food cans, and household items. Some of the boardinghouse platforms and privy pits might harbor buried archaeological deposits worth investigating."

Figure 6-51. Warrior Mark Mine Dump, 1961. (Figure 6-50, F4) Western History Department, Denver Public Library, X-62428)

Figure 6-52. Concentration Mill Foundation at the Warrior's Mark Mine. (Figure 6-50, F10) Note the mine dump seen in Figure 6-54. (Photograph by Author)

Figure 6-53. Brick Foundation for Boiler in the Concentration Mill. (Figure 6-50, F11) The open pit of the Warrior's Mark mine is behind the foundation. Refer to the USGS map in Figure 6-32. (Photograph by Author)

Figure 6-54. Warrior's Mark Mine Open Pit, 1961. (Figure 6-50, F1) (Western History Department, Denver Public Library, X-62430)

Figure 6-55. Warrior's Mark Mine Open Pit, (Figure 6-50, F1) 2009. (Photograph by Author)

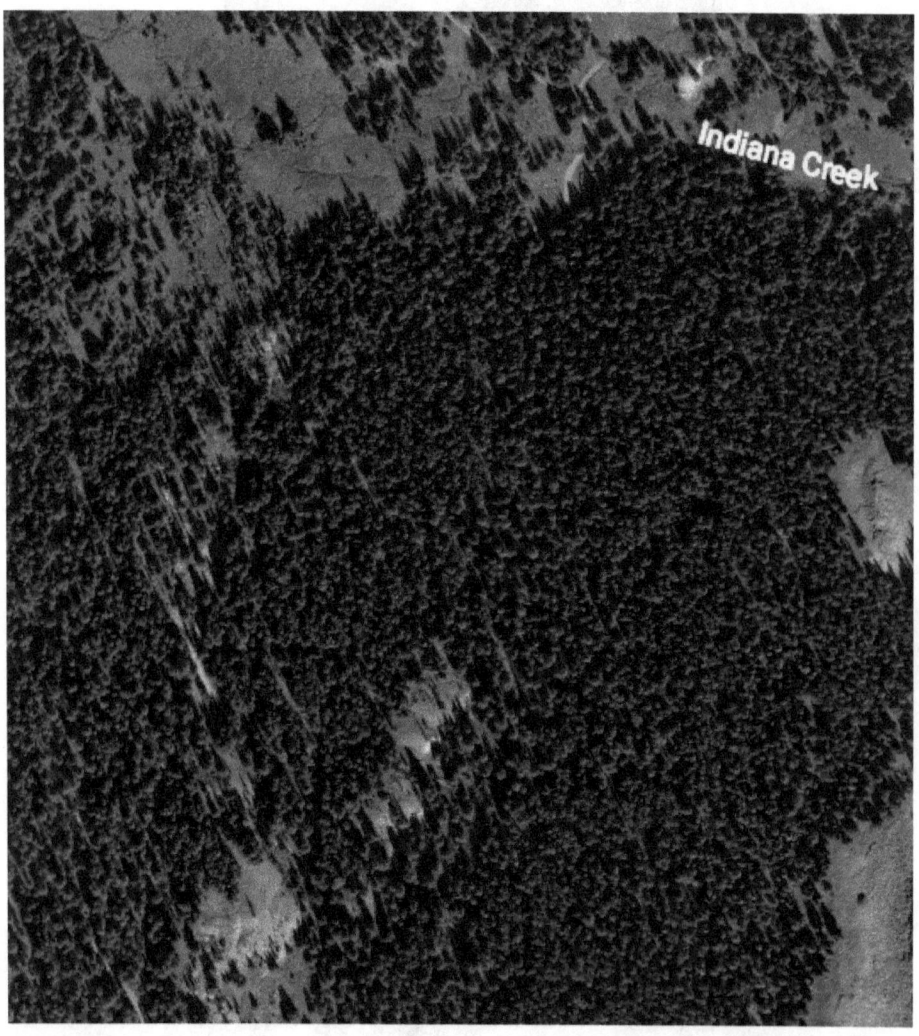

Figure 6-56. Aerial View of Dyersville and Warrior's Mark Mine, 2021. The view includes the remnants of Dyersville in the upper right and the Warrior's Mark mine in the bare area in the lower left. (Google Earth, Imagery ©2021 Maxar Technologies, U.S. Geological Survey, USDA Farm Service Agency, Map data ©2021)

Figure 6-57. Aerial View of the Dyersville Site, 2021. Remnants of buildings can be seen in the bare spot in the lower center. Note the outline of a cabin and the cabin still standing across the road in the trees. Another collapsed cabin can be seen in the bare spot in the upper right. (Google Earth, Imagery ©2021 Maxar Technologies, U.S. Geological Survey, USDA Farm Service Agency, Map data ©2021)

BIBLIOGRAPHY

Books, Articles, and Mining District Logs

Crofutt, George A. *Grip Sack Guide to Colorado*. Overland Publishing Company, 1881.

Crofutt, George A. *Grip Sack Guide to Colorado*. Overland Publishing Company, 1885.

Daugherty, John. *Cultural Resource Inventories for Summit County, Colorado, Part II, Survey of Historic Mines and Mining Camps – Swan River and French Creek*. Summit Historical Society, 1974.

Fiester, Mark. *Blasted Beloved Breckenridge*. Boulder, Colorado: Pruett Publishing Company, 1973.

Singewald, Quentin D. *Geology and Ore Deposits of the Upper Blue River Area, Summit County, Colorado*. Geological Survey Bulletin 970. United States Government Printing Office, Washington, 1951.

Wolle, Muriel Sibell. *Stampede to Timberline*, 1949.

Wolle, Muriel Sibell. *Timberline Tailings*, 1977.

Newspapers and Magazines

1. The website, Colorado Historic Newspapers Collection at https://www.coloradohistoricnewspapers.org

    a. *Summit County Journal*, 1891 to 1909 and 1914 to 1923, Breckenridge, Colorado
    b. *Breckenridge Bulletin*, 1899 to 1909, Breckenridge, Colorado
    c. *Summit County Journal and Breckenridge Bulletin*, 1909 to 1914, Breckenridge, Colorado
    d. Miscellaneous other historic Colorado newspapers

2. *Colorado Postal Historia*n, Volume 16, Number 1, August, 2000

Other Sources

Bureau of Land Management, Lakewood, Colorado

Colorado School of Mines, Arthur Lakes Library, Golden, Colorado

Colorado State Archives, Denver, Colorado

Denver Public Library, Western History Section, Denver, Colorado

Breckenridge History Archives, Breckenridge, Colorado

History Colorado, Denver, Colorado

Summit County Clerk and Recorder's Office, Breckenridge, Colorado

Summit Historical Society Archives, Dillon, Colorado

INDEX

Adair, John S.: 23, 24
Angels Rest: 97-101, 131, 132, 135
Bemrose, William: 20, 26, 34
Bissell, Gaylord G.: 23, 24
Bloomfield, J.M.: 10, 11
Bond, R.L.: 16, 21, 23, 24, 28, 31, 32
Brooks, Ble: 48, 49
Brown, Silas: 48, 49
Columbine Vein/ Shaft: 118-121, 125, 127, 141-143
Conger, Diantha: 70
Conger, Samuel Patterson: 67, 73
Dyer, Father John Lewis: 36, 87-95
El Dorado Mill: 49-55, 57, 62
Hoosier Pass: 7, 10, 14, 16, 20, 27, 29, 30, 36, 46, 47, 50
Iliff, William H.: 19
Jones, Samuel G.: 10
Krigbaum, Jerry: 68, 97, 98, 101
Lechner, George W.: 48, 49
McCollough, Canada: 33, 48, 49
Mineral City: 11
Monte Cristo Gulch: 46, 47, 49, 51, 54, 62, 82
Monte Cristo Mine: 50, 53, 82
Morrison Mining District: 23
Mount Quandary (Peak): 46-48
Muhlebach, Peter: 19
Nolan, John: 19
Peabody, Lelon: 19
Peruvian Mining District: 14, 47
Pollock Mining District: 23, 28, 32, 33, 47, 48, 82
Pollock, W.P.: 20
Poznansky, Felix: 20, 30
Silver City: 11, 14, 23, 24
Silver Lake Mining District: 16, 18-23, 25, 28, 30-33, 37, 47
Silver Ore City: 11

Silverthorn, Marshal: 19
Sisler, John W.: 19, 20
Snowdrift Mine/Shaft/Tunnel/ Vein/Placer: 103, 104, 109-112, 117, 127, 134, 141
Spaulding, Ruben R.: 18-20, 33
Stahl, Ezra: 20
The Crystal Lake Mining Company: 26, 36
Warren, Dr. C.E.: 53, 82
Warrior's Mark Mill: 106-108, 113, 115
Warrior's Mark Mine/Lode: 86, 88, 90-93, 101, 103-106, 109, 113-127, 134, 146-148, 151-154
Warrior's Mark Mining Company: 106, 109, 115, 117, 120, 124, 148
Welch, Enoch: 16, 21-25

About the Authors

Bill Fountain

Bill Fountain grew up in Southern California where he began working in the tire business while still in high school and eventually became part-owner of 23 Big O Tires stores. He and his wife, Jeanne, moved to Denver in 1987 when he was a vice-president of Big O Tires, Inc. In 1988, he purchased several of the Big O Tires stores in the Denver metro area. Although he sold his last three tire stores in December, 2009, Bill still does some consulting for other Big O Tires dealers.

In 1988, after he and Jeanne purchased a home in Breckenridge, Bill began spending his summers investigating old cabins, mines, and ghost towns and collecting books and photos. He teams with Rich Skovlin, Maureen Nicholls, and Rick Hague exploring backcountry sites. Bill spent many hours looking through records in the Summit County Courthouse in Breckenridge; the Bureau of Land Management Archives in Lakewood; the Federal Center in Lakewood; the Colorado School of Mines, Arthur Lakes Library in Golden; History Colorado; and the Denver Public Library—as well as reading historic newspapers on the Colorado Historic Newspapers website. He has transcribed over 3,500 pages of Breckenridge mining history and has a collection of more than 3,500 digitized photographs from the 1860s to 1980s. During the summer months, Bill gives special presentations and leads tours for the Summit Historical Society, Breckenridge History (previously Breckenridge Heritage Alliance), and the Frisco Historic Park & Museum.

Bill and Jeanne traveled to Hawaii in 1969 on their honeymoon spending time in Honolulu, Kauai, and in Kailua Kona on the Big Island. They returned several times to Kona in the 1970s and 1980s. In 1994, they purchased a time share at Kona Coast Resort, spending five weeks there each year. In 2003, they purchased a small condo; and in 2005, they upgraded to a large townhouse. In January, 2010, now fully retired, they purchased a home where they spend eight to nine months a year.

Even while in Hawaii, Bill continues his research on Breckenridge history. He and Jeanne return to their home in Highlands Ranch for the summers to be near their children and grandchildren. They rent a place in Summit County for two months each summer as Bill continues exploring the fascinating history of Summit County.

Bill has worked on special research projects for local authors, Mary Ellen Gilliland and Dr. Sandra Mather, Breckenridge History, Summit Historical Society, and the Breckenridge History Archives.

In 2014, Bill received the prestigious Theobald Award from Breckenridge History for his contributions to the preservation of Breckenridge's history.

In 2023, Bill received a lifetime membership to the Summit Historical Society.

Dr. Sandra F. Pritchard Mather

Dr. Sandra F. Pritchard Mather is a *professor emerita* in the Department of Earth and Space Sciences at West Chester University in Pennsylvania where she taught geology and meteorology before retiring in May, 1999. Since coming to Summit County in 1980 to complete her doctoral dissertation for the University of Oregon, she has written many books about the geologic, geographic, and historic landscapes of the county and those who lived here from 1859 until the turn of the century: *Southern Summit, A Geographer's Perspective; Roadside Summit, Part I, the Natural Landscape; Roadside Summit, Part II, the Human Landscape; Dillon, Denver, and the Dam; Men, Mining, and Machines; Behind Swinging Doors, the Saloons of Breckenridge and Summit County, Colorado—1859 to 1900; Golden Gulches, Hydraulic Mining in and around Breckenridge, Colorado; Summit County*, part of the Arcadia Images of America series; *Frisco and the Ten Mile Canyon*, also part of the Arcadia Images of America series; *They weren't all Prostitutes and Gamblers, the Women of Summit County from 1859 to the Turn of the Century; Historic Footprints, A Picture Book for Young Readers*; with Rick Hague, *Windows to the Past*, and with Bob Schoppe, the *Narrow-Gauge Railroads of Summit County*, part of the Arcadia Images of Rail series. Sandie is co-author with Bill Fountain of the *Chasing the Dream* series, *Chasing the Bad Guys, Enforcing the Law in Breckenridge, Colorado, Town Marshals 1881-1923*, and *Country Boy Mine, Breckenridge, Colorado, 1881-1994*.

About the Authors

Sandie spent summers in Summit County leading tours and presenting special programs for the Summit Historical Society, the Frisco Historic Park & Museum, and Breckenridge History. In 2013, Sandie received the prestigious Theobald Award from Breckenridge History for her contributions to the preservation of Breckenridge's history. She is a former president and life member of the Summit Historical Society.

www.ingramcontent.com/pod-product-compliance
Lightning Source LLC
Chambersburg PA
CBHW071608170426

43196CB00034B/2231